"Wisdom That Transforms. Action That Lasts."

The Get Wisdom Commitment

At Get Wisdom Publishing we believe that true wisdom has the power to transform lives. Our mission is to equip readers with timeless insights and practical tools that inspire growth, guide decisions, and empower purposeful living. We don't just inform—we empower.

Our books combine profound understanding with real-life application, enabling readers to unlock their potential and navigate life's challenges with clarity and confidence. With each step guided by wisdom, we help you create lasting change and live the life you deserve.

When wisdom meets purpose, transformation follows.

Make your heart the dwelling place of God.

Copyright

ISBN 978-1-952359-71-2   (paperback)
ISBN 978-1-952359-72-9   (ebook)

This book is available as an audiobook on our Amazon Jesus Follower Series page:	

Unlock Biblical Wisdom and Transform Your Faith

**For more information
about the Jesus Follower Bible Study Series:**
https://getwisdompublishing.com/jesus-follower-series/

Make your heart the dwelling place of God.

Jesus Follower Bible Study Series

The HEART Requirements of a Jesus Follower

Follow with all your heart, mind, body, and soul!

Stephen H Berkey

GET**WISDOM**
P U B L I S H I N G

This book is available as an audiobook on our Amazon Jesus Follower Series page:

Free PDF

Living Wisely

The Life Planning Guide

A Quick-Start Guide to Purposeful Living and Wise Decisions!

Discover the five life domains: purpose, people, principles, productivity, and perspective. Wisdom is the ability to apply truth and logic to real-life decisions and produce good outcomes. It influences your choices and will produce action that lasts. Consider and apply the five practical wisdom principles for daily living. (6 pages)

Free PDF: https://getwisdompublishing.com/resource-registration/

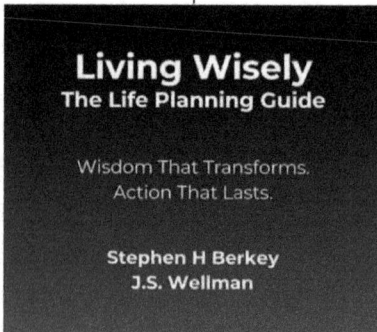

Living Wisely
The Life Planning Guide

Wisdom That Transforms.
Action That Lasts.

Stephen H Berkey
J.S. Wellman

Free PDF

Five Practical Principles For Life

When wisdom meets purpose, transformation follows.

Free PDF
Wise Decision-Making
[Get the ebook version for 99 cents]

You can make good choices.

This free resource provides a project-oriented perspective and gives ten detailed steps to analyze issues/problems to determine a solution. (26 pages)

Good decisions expand your horizons. Don't allow the fear of decision-making paralyze your ability to make good choices. Think through the reasonable alternatives and move forward. When your eyes are on the goal, making good decisions is easier.

Free PDF: https://getwisdompublishing.com/resource-registration/

Kindle ebook for 99 cents: https://www.amazon.com/dp/B09SYGWRVL/

Ebook

Free PDF

Make Thoughtful Decisions!
Good decisions expand your horizons.

Make your heart the dwelling place of God.

The Jesus Follower Journey

Jesus Follower Bible Study Series

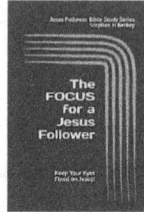

The Jesus Follower Bible Study Series will provide you with a complete description of the nature, characteristics, obligations, commitments, and responsibilities of a true Jesus follower.

Go to our Amazon Book Series page for your copy:
https://www.amazon.com/dp/B0DHP39P5J

The RELATIONSHIP CHARACTERISTICS of a Jesus Follower:
Are you right with God?
The ONE ANOTHER INSTRUCTIONS to a Jesus Follower:
Are you right with one another?
The WORSHIP of a Jesus Follower:
Is your worship acceptable or in vain?
The PRAYER of a Jesus Follower:
What Scripture says about unleashing the power of God.
The DANGERS of SIN for a Jesus Follower:
God HATES sin! He abhors sin!
The FOCUS for a Jesus Follower:
Keep your eyes fixed on Jesus!
The HEART Requirements of a Jesus Follower:
Follow with all your heart, mind, body, and soul!
The COMMITMENTS of a Jesus Follower:
Practical Christian living and discipleship.
The OBEDIENCE Requirements for a Jesus Follower:
Ignore at your own risk!

A related book to this series is, *Effective Life Change: Applying Biblical Wisdom to Live Your Best Life!* This book offers a practical and powerful guide to help navigate life's challenges.

Table of Contents

Effective Life Change

Applying Biblical Wisdom to Live Your Best Life!

Why Read This Book?

- Transform Your life with Biblical Wisdom.
- Cultivate Practical Wisdom in Your life.
- Navigate Life with a Perspective on Biblical Truth.
- Unlock the Proverbs of the Bible to Live Your Best Life.
- Change and Transform Your life.

Practical Application: These aren't theology or religious discussions, they're practical tools for everyday living.

Get Your Copy Today!

https://www.amazon.com/dp/1952359732
Available in Hardcover, Paperback, Kindle, and Audiobook.

Message From the Author

Dear Fellow Christ follower,

Welcome to a journey of faith and discovery.

As the author of this Bible study series, I am excited about the future because I believe this book provides the potential to transform lives, deepen our understanding of God's Word, and ignite a desire within us—a fire that draws us into the presence of our God.

Why read the Jesus Follower Series?

Deeper Roots: We all long for roots that run deep—roots anchored in truth, love, and purpose. In this series, we'll dig into the bedrock of Scripture, unearthing spiritual principles that will guide us in our faith journey.

Authentic Discipleship: Being a Jesus follower isn't about rituals or a superficial commitment. It's about walking the narrow path, picking up your cross, and living a life that loves God, follows Jesus, and loves one another. We will explore what it means to be authentic disciples.

Unveiling Mysteries: God is a source of mysteries and His Word is waiting to be discovered. Together we will examine and encounter the living Word—the One who breathes life into every syllable.

Community and Connection: We are not meant to walk this path alone. As you read, imagine joining a global community of fellow seekers. We will discuss, question, and grow together. Our shared journey will enrich us all. I encourage you to gather friends to join you in this journey.

Expected Benefits:

Renewed Passion: Prepare yourself to wake up each morning with a renewed passion for God's Word. These studies will ignite your hunger for truth and draw you into deeper relationship with the Author of Life.

Practical Application: These aren't theoretical discussions; they're practical tools for everyday living. Expect to see real-life changes—whether it's in your relationships, commitment, or prayer life.

Spiritual Resilience: Life's storms will come, but armed with the insights from God's Word, you can stand firm. Your faith will weather trials, doubts, and uncertainties. You will emerge stronger and more resilient.

Joyful Obedience: As we explore the nature of discipleship, you'll discover that obedience isn't a burden—it's a joy. The path of obedience leads to peace, and you'll find yourself saying, "Yes, Lord!" with newfound delight.

Let's Begin!

So, turn the page. Dive into the first chapter. Let the words seep into your soul. And remember, you're not alone—we're on this pilgrimage together. May these books be more than ink on paper; may they be stepping stones toward a life that leads to eternity. Amen!

"We believe applied wisdom empowers life change. Our books provide clarity, inspiration, and tools to equip readers to live their best life."

My prayer is that you will

Be tenacious like Job
Walk like Enoch
Believe like Abraham
Wrestle like Jacob
Dress like Joseph
Lead like Moses
Conquer like Deborah
Be fearless like Shamgar
Inspire like Josuha
Influence like Esther
Dance like David
Ask like Jabez
Have the faith of Daniel
Pray like Elijah
Trust like Elisha
Commit like Isaiah
Be courageous like Benaiah
Rebuild like Nehemiah
Be obedient like Hosea
Be zealous like Zacchaeus
Surrender like Mary
Stand firm like Stephen
Speak like Peter
Seize opportunities like Philip
Submit like Paul
Overcome like the Elect (Saints)
Worship like the 24 Elders
and
Love like Jesus

Steve

Introduction

Follow with All Your Heart, Mind, Body, and Soul!

Book Description

Embark on a transformative journey that will revolutionize your faith and ignite your passion for Christ! This powerful Bible study explores the essence of what it truly means to follow Jesus with your whole heart.

Discover the life-changing power of wholehearted devotion as you:

• Uncover the biblical meaning of the heart and its pivotal role in your spiritual journey.
• Learn how God can transform even the most hardened or broken hearts.
• Explore real-life examples of faith in action through compelling biblical narratives.
• Gain practical insights on integrating your faith into every aspect of your life.

Through eight engaging lessons, you'll examine:

1. The call to wholehearted commitment.
2. The importance and challenges of the heart.
3. God's power to change your heart.
4. Actions that require your whole heart.
5. The transformative impact of giving your all.
6. Divine encounters that shape your faith.
7. The blind man's journey from darkness to light.
8. The crippled man's leap of faith.

Perfect for individual reflection or group study, this book offers:

• Thought-provoking questions that challenge you to examine your own heart.
• Practical applications to help you live out your faith daily.
• Encouragement and hope for those seeking a deeper relationship with God.

Whether you're a new believer or a seasoned Christian, this study will equip you to:

• Love God with all your heart, mind, body, and soul.
• Overcome obstacles that hinder your spiritual growth.
• Experience the satisfying life found in undivided allegiance to Christ.

Don't settle for a lukewarm faith! Embrace the call to follow Jesus with everything you are. Get ready to be challenged, inspired, and equipped to live a life that truly honors God.

Are you prepared to unleash the full potential of your faith? Your journey to wholehearted devotion can begin here.

Group Discussion or Individual Study

These studies can be done individually or in a small discussion group. An important value of the study is in the discussion questions. We all see life differently and the thoughts and ideas shared in a group will often lead to a richer understanding of the Scripture. We recommend doing these studies in a group, if possible.

Format of Lessons

The format of the lessons is not the same in each book. We chose a format that best fit the material.

We Reap What We Sow!

In a number of his proverbs, King Solomon suggests that doing what is right is to be preferred over evil. King Solomon was known world-wide for his great wisdom. He wrote and recorded many proverbs recognized for their practical insight and wisdom. He describes the nature of righteousness as being immovable and that it will stand above evil.

Is your desire for doing what is "right" rooted deeply or is it planted in shallow soil that can easily be washed away? Solomon indicated that the wicked would ultimately be overthrown and that the righteous would survive because their character had roots that were deep and impossible to dislodge.

Solomon argued that it was better to be on the side of the righteous. The reasoning is the same as the man who builds his house, business, or life on rock versus sand. If we build on sand (questionable ways) then our hopes and plans will never stand up against the storms of life. If we build on rock (character, commitment, and obedience) our plans will hold firm.

We do reap what we sow and if we sow badly because we have rejected what is right, the wise counsel of friends, or our core values, we will reap the negative consequences. Those who think they know everything frequently reject wisdom and follow their own plans and schemes.

Choices produce consequences
which direct the course of life.
Consequences shape lives.
Therefore, count the cost!

Lesson 1
Wholehearted Commitment

"The essence of commitment is the ability
to stick with something long after
the initial excitement is gone."
Stephen Covey

INTRODUCTION

Do you remember what Solomon asked for when God
wanted to know what He should give him? If you are like
me, you would probably say wisdom. Rather than asking
for power or material things, he asked for two things.
What did Solomon ask for that ultimately made him one of
the wisest men ever to live? He asked for a *discerning
heart* in order to do two things: (1) govern his people, and
(2) distinguish between right and wrong.

*As Solomon grew old, his wives turned his heart after other
gods, and his heart was not fully devoted to the LORD his
God, as the heart of David his father had been.*
1 Kings 11:4 NIV

And although most people think God gave Solomon
wisdom, He actually gave him "a wise and discerning
heart." (1 Kings 3:12) You may think I am splitting hairs to
suggest that there is a significant difference between
receiving wisdom and receiving a discerning heart because
in 1 Kings 10:24 the author says that:

*The whole world sought audience with Solomon
to hear the wisdom God had put in his <u>heart</u>.* NIV

Since I assume God wants us to know and understand truth, I believe there is something important that God wants us to know about the "heart." It would have been possible to simply say that Solomon was given wisdom or was made wise, but that is not what the Bible describes. It says that his <u>heart</u> was made wise.

I probably would never have noticed this, except that one night the leader of my Men's Bible Study happened to mention that the word "heart" was used 710 times in the Bible. I came home thinking that if one word is used that often it had to be very important. I was aware that the word love was used about 550 times in the NIV, so if "heart" is used even more, I wanted to find out exactly what the Bible said about the word. I knew it said I had to believe in my heart if I wanted to be saved (Romans 10:9).

The word "heart" is used 569 times in the NIV and "hearts" is used another 208 times. This is compared to 156 times the word "mind(s)" is used. Obviously the heart and its nature is an important and even critical concept in our relationship to Christ. (For more insight into the nature of what the Bible says about the "mind" or "thoughts" refer to Appendix A at the end of the book.)

The word "heart" is used in various different ways and contexts in Scripture. Here are seven examples:

1. **The heart is the seat of our emotions and desires.** In many passages "heart" refers to the center of human emotions and feelings. It includes love, joy, sorrow, and other deep emotions. Proverbs 4:23 says, "*Keep your heart with all vigilance, for from it flow the springs of life.*" (ESV) We will discuss this verse more

fully in the next lesson.

2. **The heart is the intellectual and spiritual center of our soul.** The heart is portrayed as the center of understanding and spiritual insight. In Psalm 119:11, the psalmist declares, "*I have stored up your word in my heart, that I might not sin against you.*" (ESV) Thus the heart is where spiritual truths are internalized and decisions are made.

3. **The heart is where we make moral and ethical decisions.** The heart represents the innermost being of a person where intentions and motives are judged. Jesus often addressed matters of the heart in this sense, such as in Matthew 5:8. (NIV) He said, "*Blessed are the pure in heart, for they will see God.*" This is where purity, moral integrity, and sincere devotion to God reside.

4. **The heart is where our relationship with God is established and maintained.** The heart must be central to our relationship with God. It is where faith lives and where one responds to God's call. Romans 10:9-10 (NIV) states, "*If you declare with your mouth, 'Jesus is Lord,' and believe in your heart that God raised him from the dead, you will be saved.*" Belief in the heart is necessary to ensure genuine belief in God.

5. **The heart is where we solidify our unity and relationship with God.** In Deuteronomy 6:5 (NIV) Moses commanded the people to "*Love the Lord your God with all your heart and with all your soul and with all your strength.*" Loving God from our heart implies complete devotion and sincerity.

6. **The heart is also used to denote intensity and determination.** Sometimes a reference to "heart" is

used to denote determination, courage, or perseverance. In 1 Samuel 17:32 (NIV) David says to Saul, "*Let no one lose heart on account of this Philistine; your servant will go and fight him.*" Here, "lose heart" refers to losing courage or resolve.

7. **Finally, the heart is a physical organ**. The Bible occasionally refers to the heart as the physical organ responsible for pumping blood. But even in these situations, the reference may have metaphorical implications. For example, in Acts 14:17 (NIV), Paul speaks of God "*filling our hearts with food and gladness,*" using the physical heart to symbolize satisfaction and joy in a spiritual sense.

We can observe in these various uses that the, "heart" is used to consistently represent deep aspects of human experience, emotion, thoughts, intentions, spiritual condition, and even our relationship with God. Its usage reflects the complexity of our human nature and the depth of God's interaction with His people. Thus, the heart represents the core of a person's identity and is crucial in the Biblical context of understanding our relationship with God and interacting with one another.

Doing something "with all our heart" means that we do it completely, sincerely, and diligently. We are fully devoted, determined, and enthusiastic about it. There is no hesitation or reservation about it; we have a complete earnest commitment. We bring every area of our life under the lordship of Christ (1 Corinthians 10:31; Colossians 3:17). This means we integrate our faith into all areas of life including our work, relationships, hobbies, pleasure, etc.

INNER BEING

In addition to the term "heart" the Bible uses several other terms and phrases that convey a similar meaning of the inner person or the core of one's being. It is the seat of emotions, thoughts, and intentions that produce our core personality.

Q1. What do we learn about the heart in the following passages?

Romans 7:22 *For in my inner being I delight in God's law;* NIV

Ephesians 3:16 *I pray that out of his glorious riches he may strengthen you with power through his Spirit in your inner being . . .* NIV

1 Peter 3:4 *Instead, it should be that of your inner self, the unfading beauty of a gentle and quiet spirit, which is of great worth in God's sight.* NIV

Psalms 51:6 *Surely you desire truth in the inner parts; you teach me wisdom in the inmost place.* NIV
Psalms 139:13 *For you formed my inward parts; you knitted me together in my mother's womb.* ESV

HEART AND SOUL COMBINED

We have seen that the heart is described as the inner being or self, but there are a number of other terms used to describe this concept. One of the more interesting is the connection to the term "soul." Merriam-Webster defines soul as a person or "a person's total self." The term soul(s) appears 98 times in the NIV translation and 293 in the ESV translation where it is used more frequently instead of heart, compared to other translations. The following two verses are representative of its use:

> **Psalms 42:1** *As a deer pants for flowing streams, so pants my <u>soul</u> for you, O God.* ESV

> **Matthew 10:28** *And do not fear those who kill the body but cannot kill the <u>soul</u>. Rather fear him who can destroy both <u>soul</u> and body in hell.* ESV

Probably one of the more important facts about the use of the word "soul" is that it is used to describe a number of different perspectives relative to the heart or inner life of man. It is often combined together with "heart" in the same verse to represent man's inner core or being.

Q2. What does Scripture tell us about <u>seeking</u> the Lord and the soul (heart) in the following passages?

Deuteronomy 4:29 *But if from there you seek the LORD your God, you will find him if you look for him with all your heart and with all your soul.* NIV

2 Chronicles 15:12 *They entered into a covenant to seek the LORD, the God of their fathers, with all their heart and soul.* NIV

Q3. What does Scripture tell us about <u>loving</u> the Lord and the soul (heart) in the following passages?

Deuteronomy 6:5 *Love the LORD your God with all your heart and with all your soul and with all your strength.* NIV

Deuteronomy 13:3 *you must not listen to the words of that prophet or dreamer. The LORD your God is testing you to find out whether you love him with all your heart and with all your soul.* NIV

Matthew 22:37 Jesus replied: 'Love the Lord your God with all your heart and with all your soul and with all your mind.' NIV [also Mk 12:30; Lk 10:27]

Q4. What does Scripture tell us about <u>serving</u> the Lord and the heart and soul in the following passage?

Deuteronomy 10:12 *And now, O Israel, what does the LORD your God ask of you but to fear the LORD your God, to walk in all his ways, to love him, to serve the LORD your God with all your heart and with all your soul,* NIV [Also Deuteronomy 11:13 and Joshua 22:5]

21

Q5. What does Scripture tell us about <u>obeying</u> the Lord and the heart soul in the following passages?

Deuteronomy 26:16 *The LORD your God commands you this day to follow these decrees and laws; carefully observe them with all your heart and with all your soul.* NIV

2 Kings 23:3 *The king stood by the pillar and renewed the covenant in the presence of the LORD – to follow the LORD and keep his commands, regulations and decrees with all his heart and all his soul, thus confirming the words of the covenant written in this book. Then all the people pledged themselves to the covenant.* NIV

Q6. What does Scripture tell us about <u>repentance</u> and the heart and soul in the following passage?

Deuteronomy 30:10 *if you obey the LORD your God and keep his commands and decrees that are written in this Book of the Law and turn to the LORD your God with all your heart and with all your soul.* NIV
[see also 1 Kings 8:48; 2 Chronicles 6:38]
Ans:

Q7. What else does Scripture tell us about the <u>soul</u> (heart) in the following?

Psalms 19:7 *The law of the LORD is perfect, reviving the soul. . . .* NIV

Psalms 62:1 *My soul finds rest in God alone; my salvation comes from him.* NIV

1 Peter 2:11 *Dear friends, I urge you, as aliens and strangers in the world, to abstain from sinful desires, which war against your soul.* NIV

Ps 130:5-6 *I wait for the LORD, my soul waits, and in his word I put my hope. 6 My soul waits for the Lord more than watchmen wait for the morning . . .* NIV

Proverbs 22:5 *In the paths of the wicked lie thorns and snares, but he who guards his soul stays far from them.* NIV

OTHER DESCRIPTIONS OF THE "HEART"

SPIRIT: Heart is also associated with the word "spirit" in referencing the individual:

Psalms 51:10 *Create in me a clean <u>heart</u>, O God, and renew a right <u>spirit</u> within me.* ESV

Ezekiel 36:26-27 *And I will give you a new heart, and a new <u>spirit</u> I will put within you. And I will remove the <u>heart</u> of stone from your flesh and give you a heart of flesh. 27 And I will put my Spirit within you, and cause you to walk in my statutes and be careful to obey my rules.* ESV

MIND: There are two other well-known verses that use another term: mind. In most cases the word mind refers to our thinking or mental facilities, but on occasion mind is used to represent our inner being:

Romans 12:2 *Do not be conformed to this world, but be transformed by the renewal of your <u>mind</u>, that by testing you may discern what is the will of God, what is good and acceptable and perfect.* ESV

Philippians 4:7-8 *And the peace of God, which surpasses all understanding, will guard your hearts and your <u>minds</u> in Christ Jesus. Finally, brothers, whatever is true, whatever is honorable, whatever is just, whatever is pure, whatever is lovely, whatever is commendable, if there is any excellence, if there is anything worthy of praise, <u>think about these things</u>.* ESV

CONSCIENCE: The word "conscience" is also used (29 times in the ESV) to describe our inner self:

Romans 2:15 *They show that the work of the law is written on their hearts, while their <u>conscience</u> also bears witness, and their conflicting thoughts accuse or even excuse them* ESV

> **1 Timothy 1:5** *The aim of our charge is love that issues from a pure heart and a good <u>conscience</u> and a sincere faith.* ESV

All these terms in the Bible convey various aspects of the inner person. Therefore it is not surprising that they reflect the complexity and depth of human emotions, thoughts, intentions, and spiritual life. They are intended to describe the entirety or center core of our being.

THE HEART IS THE CORE OF MAN

So, the question is, "Does the heart really represent the true core of man?" Does the Bible actually define this place within us in a way that we can conclude without any doubt that "the heart" really represents our true inner self? There are several passages that come close to describing our hearts in this way. For example:

Proverbs 4:23 *Above all else, guard your heart, for it is the <u>wellspring of life</u>.* NLT

Proverbs 17:3 The crucible for silver and the furnace for gold, but <u>the LORD tests the heart</u>. NIV

Proverbs 21:2 All a man's ways seem right to him, but the <u>LORD weighs the heart</u>. NIV

Psalm 16:7 I will praise the LORD, who counsels me; <u>even at night my heart instructs me.</u> NIV

In addition the prophets of the Old Testament had a great deal to say about the nature of the heart. Zechariah may have summarized it best when he said: *"They made their hearts as hard as flint and would not listen to the law or to the words that the LORD Almighty had sent by his Spirit through the earlier prophets. So the LORD Almighty was very angry."* (Zechariah 7:12 NIV)

It seems obvious that the heart represents the core of our existence. It defines our true self. It encompasses all of who we really are, both good and bad. It is the center where our self or being is truly defined. The heart is the ultimate source for love, obedience, repentance, hatred, wickedness, and sin. All decisions or actions relative to God must come from the heart to be valid.

For example, we must believe from the heart to be saved (Romans 10:9-10), and our greatest duty is to love God with all our hearts (Matthew 22:37). Although evil and wickedness come from the heart (Mark 7:20-23; Romans 1:24-25), God knows our heart (Psalm 44:21; Acts 15:8; 1 John 3:20c), thus we are warned to guard our hearts (Proverbs 4:23). If we want to approach God we must have sincere hearts, free from guilt (Hebrews 10:22). And, lastly and most importantly, our heart is the dwelling place of Christ (Ephesians 3:17).

If the heart is that place in our existence where truth exists and the place that represents our true feelings, true belief, and true self, then, this is a place we must know about and totally understand. It is a place that must be well understood, cultivated, and developed because it is the place that counts with God. Many of us blithely say or hope that God knows we really didn't mean it when evil, wickedness, or sin rears its ugly head in our lives. But that ugliness comes from the heart: *"From their callous hearts comes iniquity; the evil conceits of their minds know no limits."* (Psalms 73:7 NIV)

THE HOLY SPIRIT

God has also given us the Holy Spirit so His divine presence resides in our hearts:

> **2 Corinthians 1:22** . . . *set his seal of ownership on us, and put his <u>Spirit in our hearts</u> as a deposit, guaranteeing what is to come.* NIV

> **Galatians 4:6** *Because you are sons, God sent the <u>Spirit of his Son</u> <u>into our hearts</u>, the Spirit who calls out, "Abba, Father."* NIV

> **Ephesians 3:17** . . . *so that <u>Christ may dwell in your hearts</u> through faith* . . . NIV

Q8 What do the following passages say the Holy Spirit will do in our hearts?

Colossians 4:8 *I am sending him to you for the express purpose that you may know about our circumstances and that he may encourage your hearts.* NIV

1 Thessalonians 3:13 *May he strengthen your hearts so that you will be blameless and holy in the presence of our God and Father when our Lord Jesus comes with all his holy ones.* NIV

2 Thessalonians 2:16-17 *Now may our Lord Jesus Christ himself, and God our Father, who loved us and gave us eternal comfort and good hope through grace, 17 comfort*

your hearts and establish them in every good work and word. ESV

2 Thessalonians 3:5 *May the Lord <u>direct your hearts into God's love</u> and Christ's perseverance.* NIV

The Bible mentions instances where God encourages the hearts of men, offering comfort, strength, and assurance in various situations. In Psalm 27:14 we are encouraged in trials when we are told to wait for the Lord and be strong. We are to take courage in knowing that the Lord is near. Isaiah gives us a similar message in Isaiah 41:10 where he says "*fear not for I am with you.*" The prophet goes on to say that God will help us with His righteous right hand. Deuteronomy 31:8 says, "*It is the Lord who goes before you. He will be with you; he will not leave you or forsake you. Do not fear or be dismayed.*" ESV

Q9. What do you learn in the following two passages?

Matthew 10:28-31 *And do not fear those who kill the body but cannot kill the soul. Rather fear him who can destroy both soul and body in hell. 29 Are not two sparrows sold for a penny? And not one of them will fall to the ground apart from your Father. 30 But even the hairs of your head are all numbered. 31 Fear not, therefore; you are of more value than many sparrows.* ESV

2 Corinthians 1:3-4 *Blessed be the God and Father of our Lord Jesus Christ, the Father of mercies and God of all comfort, 4 who comforts us in all our affliction, so that we may be able to comfort those who are in any affliction, with the comfort with which we ourselves are comforted by God.* ESV

These passages demonstrate God's heart of compassion and encouragement toward His people. He provides peace to those who trust in Him, often through His Word, His presence, and His promises. God's encouragement serves to uplift and sustain us in times of fear and uncertainty, reinforcing our faith and dependence on Him.

CONCLUSION

The Bible paints an extensive portrait of man's relationship with God. Central to this relationship are the "heart" and "soul." These terms serve as metaphors of our inner core, the wellspring of thoughts, desires, intentions, and motivations. While the Bible uses other terms like spirit, mind, and conscience, the "heart" often stands as a unifying concept for this inner self.

There are several very important concepts we should lock into our memories:

The Dwelling Place of God: The Bible portrays the heart as the potential sanctuary of God. Passages like Ephesians 3:17 speak of God desiring to "*make his home in your hearts through faith.*" A transformed heart becomes a hospitable environment for the Holy Spirit to reside and work in our lives.

The Source of Decisions and Actions: The Bible makes a clear connection between the inner state of the heart and outward actions. Proverbs 4:23 states, "*For out of the heart comes evil thoughts, murder, adultery, sexual immorality, theft, false testimony, slander.*" Our hearts are like factories, where the raw materials of our thoughts and desires are processed and eventually manifest in our deeds and good works.

The Seat of Sin: The Bible acknowledges the inherent sinfulness of humanity, informing us that it resides within the core of our being. Romans 3:23 declares, "*for all have sinned and fall short of the glory of God.*" This sinfulness is not external but rooted in the heart. Galatians 5:19-21 confirms the ugliness of the evil in our souls.

Transformation through Repentance: Transformation goes beyond simply changing outward behavior or saying we are sorry. True repentance involves sorrow for sin and a turning away from it within the heart, often accompanied by confession and a deep desire for change (Acts 2:37-38). True repentance is required for salvation and it must come from the heart.

Faith and Love Flow from the Heart: Genuine faith in God is not simply intellectual assent but a heart-felt trust and reliance. Love for God and others is not a duty but a natural overflow of a transformed heart (1 John 4:7-8).

Obedience Begins in the Heart: When our hearts are changed, obedience to God's commands becomes a natural response out of love and gratitude, not a begrudging obligation (Deuteronomy 10:12-13). We do good deeds because our heart has been changed, not to gain right standing with God.

Throughout Scripture, we see examples of the heart's significance. King David, after his sin, pleaded with God for a "clean heart" (Psalm 51:10). The prophet Ezekiel spoke of God giving His people "a new heart" and "a new spirit" (Ezekiel 36:26). The Bible's focus on the heart highlights the importance of inner transformation. It's not enough to simply go through the motions. To truly please and obey God requires a change at the core of our being. When our hearts are transformed, we experience forgiveness, are empowered to live righteously, and then become instruments of His love in the world.

APPLICATION QUESTIONS

1. What is the heart issue you need to work on now? Be specific:

    The problem is:

    I should do the following:

2. Who could I ask to help me or hold me accountable?

3. What new core values should I establish in my life?

WHAT DO I WANT TO REMEMBER?

Enter some notes and information that you want to remember about this lesson. It might be a Scripture verse or two, something new you learned, something you want to do, something you want to change, or just something you want to be sure to remember.

Wisdom to Action
Challenge

What steps can you take to better guard and cultivate your heart this week? How will you ensure your inner being aligns more closely with God's will and truth?

Lesson 2
The Importance and Problems of the Heart

Above all else,
guard your heart,
for it is the wellspring of life.
Proverbs 4:23 World English Bible

PROVERBS 4:23

This proverb carries a deep and metaphorical meaning. "Guarding your heart" refers to the inner self where truth resides. We saw in Lesson 1 that the heart represents the core of our emotions, desires, and inner self. We must protect our innermost feelings, values, and moral compass. It means being careful about what we allow to influence us, including the relationships we pursue, the media we consume, and the thoughts we entertain.

The term "wellspring of life" is an important concept because it signifies a source of abundant supply. The NIV says, "for everything you do flows from it" Just as a wellspring is an abundant water source, the heart is the source of everything that makes us alive, including our passions, emotions, and values. It's the origin of our actions and decisions, and it shapes our character, life, and particularly our walk with God.

Proverbs 4:23 tells us to be vigilant in protecting our inner self, our values, and our emotions, as they are the source of our well-being. It's a reminder that what we allow to influence our hearts can have a profound impact on our lives. It's a call to be mindful of what we let into our hearts. We should strive to fill our hearts with good and positive influences. This will allow the heart to produce actions and decisions that lead to a fulfilling, peaceful, and righteous life.

IMPORTANCE OF THE HEART

Isaiah 29:13 may be the verse that best describes the importance of the heart. "*These people come near to me with their mouth and honor me with their lips, but their hearts are far from me. Their worship of me is made up only of rules taught by men.*" NIV

It doesn't matter what we say or the image we portray to others; what matters is the condition of our hearts.

Q1. What do we learn about the importance of the heart in the following passages?

Jeremiah 4:4 *Circumcise yourselves to the LORD, circumcise your hearts, you men of Judah and people of Jerusalem, or my wrath will break out and burn like fire because of the evil you have done – burn with no one to quench it.* NIV

Ezekiel 33:31   *My people come to you, as they usually do, and sit before you to listen to your words, but they do not put them into practice. With their mouths they express devotion, but their hearts are greedy for unjust gain.* NIV

Malachi 4:6   *He will turn the hearts of the fathers to their children, and the hearts of the children to their fathers; or else I will come and strike the land with a curse.* NIV

Psalms 14:1   *The fool says in his heart, "There is no God." They are corrupt, their deeds are vile; there is no one who does good.* NIV

Psalms 26:2   *Test me, O LORD, and try me, examine my heart and my mind . . .* NIV

Psalms 37:4   *Delight yourself in the LORD and he will give you the desires of your heart.* NIV

Proverbs 11:20   *The LORD detests men of perverse heart but he delights in those whose ways are blameless.* NIV

THE PROBLEM OF THE HEART: It is evil and sinful

General

After the fall of Adam, men's hearts became sinful.
Mankind became so bad that Genesis 6:5 (NIV) reports,
*"The LORD saw how great man's wickedness on the earth
had become, and that every inclination of the thoughts of
his heart was only evil all the time."* Fortunately, *"Noah
found favor in the eyes of the LORD."* (Genesis 6:8 NIV)
However, the flood that God sent did not eradicate all sin.
Adam's original sin was part of Noah and his family and
continues to infect the human race today.

Jeremiah may best express man's frustration: *"The heart is
deceitful above all things and beyond cure. Who can
understand it?"* (Jeremiah 17:9 NIV) Even the Apostle Paul
struggled with sin:

> **Romans 7:15, 18-19** *I do not understand what I
> do. For what I want to do I do not do, but what I
> hate I do. . . . 18 I know that nothing good lives
> in me, that is, in my sinful nature. For I have the
> desire to do what is good, but I cannot carry it
> out. 19 For what I do is not the good I want to
> do; no, the evil I do not want to do-this I keep
> on doing.* NIV

Psalms 58:2 is a damning indictment: "*No, in your underline heart
you devise injustice, and your hands mete out violence on
the earth*." (NIV) Psalm 78 is a psalm of instruction that
reminds us not to sin. The psalmist gives warnings not to
repeat Israel's sins but to remember God's grace and be
faithful. But verse 37 says their hearts were not loyal to
Him – the people were not faithful to the covenants. Later
in Psalm 95:10-11 we see:

For forty years I was angry with that generation; I said, "They are a people whose <u>hearts</u> go astray, and they have not known my ways." 11 So I declared on oath in my anger, "They shall never enter my rest." NIV

Evil Hearts

Solomon, speaking of our hearts in Ecclesiastes 9:3 NIV says, "*This is the evil in everything that happens under the sun: The same destiny overtakes all. The <u>hearts</u> of men, moreover, are full of evil and there is madness in their <u>hearts</u> while they live, and afterward they join the dead.*"

The Old Testament prophets had much to say about our stubborn hearts:

Jeremiah 3:17	the people had stubborn hearts.
Jeremiah 5:23	the people had both stubborn and rebellious hearts
Jeremiah 7:24	They followed the stubborn inclinations of their hearts.
Jeremiah 9:14	Their stubbornness resulted in the people following the Baals.

Jeremiah 11:8 tells us the result of following stubborn evil hearts: God brought on them the curses outlined in the Covenants. Jeremiah 17:9-10 sums up the heart as follows: "*The <u>heart is deceitful</u> above all things and beyond cure. Who can understand it? 10 "I the LORD search the heart and examine the mind, to reward a man according to his conduct, according to what his deeds deserve.*" NIV

The prophet Ezekiel says a great deal about the <u>adulterous hearts</u> of the people (Ezekiel 6:9) that had turned away from God and lusted after idols. Idolatry was the major sin that had plagued Israel from their beginning. Ezekiel 14:3 tells us that Israel had set up idols in their hearts, thus creating a stumbling block between them and God.

Q10. What is said about the human heart in the following passages from the New Testament?

Mark 7:21 *For from within, out of men's hearts, come evil thoughts, sexual immorality, theft, murder, adultery. . .* NIV

James 3:14 *But if you harbor bitter envy and selfish ambition in your hearts, do not boast about it or deny the truth.* NIV

Mt 15:19-20 *For out of the heart come evil thoughts, murder, adultery, sexual immorality, theft, false testimony, slander. 20 These are what make a man 'unclean'; but eating with unwashed hands does not make him 'unclean.'"* NIV

The result is that in 1 Corinthians 4:5 God says He will reveal the people's sins. He will shine His light on their sins that they think are hidden. He will expose their sinful motives. James solution for this reality is to "*Come near to God and he will come near to you. Wash your hands, you sinners, and purify your hearts, you double-minded.*" (James 4:8 NIV)

Hard and Hardened Hearts

Our actions and apathy can harden our hearts. God can and will also harden the hearts of men. He may choose to harden your heart. If He hardened the heart of Pharaoh (Exodus 4:21), why would He not harden yours when you are stubborn and openly sinful? God will do what He needs to do to accomplish His bigger plan and purposes. If our rebellion is in the way of His plans we have a serious problem. Paul reminds us in Romans 9:18, "*Therefore God has mercy on whom he wants to have mercy, and he hardens whom he wants to harden.*" NIV

Sin is the ultimate cause of our hearts being hardened. Hebrews 3:13 says, "*But encourage one another daily, as long as it is called Today, so that none of you may be hardened by sin's deceitfulness.*" (NIV) Solomon warns us to protect our hearts: *Blessed is the man who always fears the LORD, but he who hardens his heart falls into trouble.* (Proverbs 28:14 NIV)

The result of a hardened heart is devastating. Israel sought the righteousness of God but it eluded them because of their sinful conduct. They refused the way of faith. In describing this Paul says, "*What then? What Israel sought so earnestly it did not obtain, but the elect did. The others were hardened.*" (Romans 11:7 NIV)

Q11. Why do you think God hardens hearts? Isn't that unfair or interference with the free will of man?

CONCLUSION

In the Old Testament, the "heart" is often portrayed as the real core of a person, encompassing their thoughts, emotions, will, and moral center. It is the seat of decision-making and moral judgment. Proverbs 4:23 tells us to guard our hearts because it is the wellspring of life. The heart is crucial in the relationship between humanity and God. Deuteronomy 6:5 commands, "*Love the Lord your God with all your heart and with all your soul and with all your strength.*" NIV

The Old Testament also emphasizes the need for inward repentance and spiritual renewal of the heart. David pleads for a pure heart in Psalm 51. His desire for a pure heart tells us that God can purify and transform our innermost being. God desires truth in our inner being (Psalm 51:6) and He looks at the heart rather than outward appearances (1 Samuel 16:7).

In the New Testament, while the concept of the heart retains its foundational meaning from the Old Testament, it takes on additional dimensions in light of Jesus' teachings and the work of the Holy Spirit:

- **Transformation**: The New Testament emphasizes the transformation of the heart through faith in Christ and the indwelling Holy Spirit.

- **Fruit**: The heart is a place where the Holy Spirit produces spiritual fruit. Galatians 5:22-23 (NIV) lists these as "*love, joy, peace, forbearance, kindness, goodness, faithfulness, gentleness and self-control.*"

- **Faith**: The heart is instrumental in expressions of faith and trust in God.

- **Worship**: The heart plays a central role in genuine worship of God. Ephesians 5:19 encourages believers to *"sing and make music from your heart to the Lord,"* emphasizing heartfelt worship.

The heart represents the core of human existence and is the cornerstone of our relationship with God. It serves as the focus of spiritual transformation, moral decision-making, as well as relational integrity. It reflects God's desire for wholehearted devotion and obedience.

DISCUSSION QUESTIONS

1. How would you describe the importance of the "heart" to a Christian friend?

2. Would the same explanation in (1) above work for a non-Christian friend? Why? Why not?

3. Proverbs 4:23 tells us to guard our hearts. How important do you think that is? Why?

4. How do you think we can <u>practically</u> apply the advice of Proverbs 4:23 to guard our hearts? What must we do?

5. Do you believe your heart is really inherently evil (Jeremiah 17:9-10)? Why? Why not?

6. What do you think it means to serve God with <u>sincerity</u> of heart, and how can we cultivate this in our lives?

7. How does the condition of your heart affect your worship?

8. Reflecting on Jesus' teaching in Luke 6:45.
The good person out of the good treasure of his heart produces good, and the evil person out of his evil treasure produces evil, for out of the abundance of the heart his mouth speaks. ESV
Do you think your words reveal the condition of your heart?

WHAT DO I WANT TO REMEMBER?

Enter some notes and information that you want to remember about this lesson. It might be a Scripture verse or two, something new you learned, something you want to do, something you want to change, or just something you want to be sure to remember.

Wisdom to Action
Challenge

What steps can you take to better guard and cultivate your heart this week? How will you ensure your inner being aligns more closely with God's will and truth?

Lesson 3
God Can Change Your Heart

"One's heart, when one is young, is very reckless.
It takes no thought for the future, and clings
to the present as if it would last forever."
Somerset Maugham

INTRODUCTION

The Bible emphasizes the need for a change of heart in order to make life improvements. A change of heart is necessary for transformation and growth. The Scriptures reveal the need for God to work in our hearts, enabling us to live according to His will and experience genuine change.

The Bible often emphasizes that we do evil things because our hearts are evil. Jeremiah 17:9 states, *"The heart is deceitful above all things, and desperately sick; who can understand it?"* Psalm 86:11 further expresses the need for an undivided heart in order for God to change our hearts to fear His Name.

Our Christian faith changes our lives because it changes our hearts. Transformation of our hearts is made possible through the work of the Holy Spirit and the grace of God.

Q1. What do the following two passages tell us about heart change?

Matthew 6:19-21 *Do not lay up for yourselves treasures on earth, where moth and rust destroy and where thieves break in and steal, 20 but lay up for yourselves treasures in heaven, where neither moth nor rust destroys and where thieves do not break in and steal. 21 For where your treasure is, there your heart will be also.* ESV

Jeremiah 31:33 *But this is the covenant that I will make with the house of Israel after those days, declares the Lord: I will put my law within them, and I will write it on their hearts. And I will be their God, and they shall be my people.* ESV

GOD AND OUR HEARTS

If the heart is such a critical part of man's nature, then how does the Godhead relate to man's heart? What does Scripture say?

Q2. 1 Kings 8:39 confirms that God knows the hearts of men, but it also confirms another very important fact. What is it?
1 Kings 8:39 *. . . then hear from heaven, your dwelling place. Forgive and act; deal with each man according to all he does, since you know his heart (for you alone know the hearts of all men). . .* NIV

Q3. Psalm 7:9 also confirms that God knows the heart. What else does He know?

Psalms 7:9 *O righteous God, who searches minds and hearts, bring to an end the violence of the wicked and make the righteous secure.* NIV

Q4. 1 Samuel 16:7 also confirms that God knows the heart, but what other fact becomes obvious?

1 Samuel 16:7 *But the LORD said to Samuel, "Do not consider his appearance or his height, for I have rejected him. The LORD does not look at the things man looks at. Man looks at the outward appearance, but the LORD looks at the heart."* NIV

Q5. Luke 16:15 confirms that God knows our hearts, but what do we learn about "core values?"

Luke 16:15 *He said to them, "You are the ones who justify yourselves in the eyes of men, but God knows your hearts. What is highly valued among men is detestable in God's sight.* NIV

Q6. Acts 15:8 confirms that God searches the heart and it also confirms another theological fact. What is it?
Acts 15:8 *God, who knows the heart, showed that he accepted them by giving the Holy Spirit to them, just as he did to us.* NIV

Q7. What do we learn in Revelation 2:23 about judgment and our hearts?
Revelation 2:23 *I will strike her children dead. Then all the churches will know that I am he who searches hearts and minds, and I will repay each of you according to your deeds.* NIV

GOD TESTS THE HEARTS OF MEN

Jeremiah 11:20 *But, O LORD Almighty, you who judge righteously and <u>test</u> the heart and mind, let me see your vengeance upon them, for to you I have committed my cause.* NIV

1 Thessalonians 2:4 *On the contrary, we speak as men approved by God to be entrusted with the gospel. We are not trying to please men but God, who <u>tests</u> our hearts.* NIV

Throughout the Bible, there are instances where God tested the hearts of men. The purpose of these tests was to reveal and refine the true character, faith, or obedience of individuals. We are probably all familiar to some extent about how God tested Abraham in Genesis 22. God told Abraham to sacrifice his only son and Abraham followed God's commands. But Isaac was rescued by God when a substitute sacrifice was provided by God. God did the same thing for mankind by sending Jesus as the substitute sacrifice for our sins.

But it is important to recognize why God was testing Abraham. God tested him to determine if he would obey (Genesis 22:18). Abraham passed the test. God and His instructions must be revered above our own worldly desires. God was testing the condition of Abraham's heart.

You may remember that God ushered the Israelites around the wilderness for forty years. This wasn't just a time to wait while all the idol worshippers died off – He was testing their hearts:

> *And you shall remember the whole way that the Lord your God has led you these forty years in the wilderness, that he might humble you, testing you to know what was in your heart, whether you would keep his commandments or not.* (Deuteronomy 8:2 ESV)

Q8. Why do you think God was so interested in whether Israel would "keep His commandments?"

Q9. There were other examples of God's testing. Why was He testing in the following examples?

2 Chronicles 32:31 *And so in the matter of the envoys of the princes of Babylon, who had been sent to him to inquire about the sign that had been done in the land, God left him to himself, in order to test him and to know all that was in his heart.* ESV

Psalms 26:2 *Prove me, O Lord, and try me; test my heart and my mind.* ESV

James 1:2-4 *Count it all joy, my brothers, when you meet trials of various kinds, 3 for you know that the testing of your faith produces steadfastness. 4 And let steadfastness have its full effect, that you may be perfect and complete, lacking in nothing.* ESV

These passages illustrate that God tests the hearts of individuals to discern and demonstrate their obedience, faithfulness, and spiritual maturity. The testing process often reveals the true nature of one's commitment to God, either affirming their faithfulness or highlighting areas in need of repentance and growth. It serves as a means of refining and purifying believers, strengthening their trust and cementing their dependence on God.

CAN GOD CHANGE YOUR HEART?

Q10. What do we learn in the following passages about God and our hearts?

1 Samuel 10:9 *As Saul turned to leave Samuel, God changed Saul's heart, and all these signs were fulfilled that day.* NIV

Jeremiah 24:7 *I will give them a heart to know me, that I am the LORD. They will be my people, and I will be their God, for they will return to me with all their heart.* NIV

Ezekiel 36:26 *I will give you a new heart and put a new spirit in you; I will remove from you your heart of stone and give you a heart of flesh.* NIV

Deuteronomy 30:6 The LORD your God will circumcise your hearts and the hearts of your descendants . . . NIV

CONCLUSION

The Bible places tremendous importance on "heart change," a transformation in the inner most part of a person that reorients our desires and moves us toward God. This change is not merely intellectual assent to beliefs, but a fundamental shift in our allegiance relationship.

Various Scriptures throughout the Bible illustrate this concept. King David, after his adultery with Bathsheba, asked God to "Create in me a clean heart" (Psalm 51:10). Similarly, the prophet Ezekiel spoke of God giving His people "a new heart" and "a new spirit" (Ezekiel 36:26). The Bible presents the clear message that a genuine change of heart is essential for pleasing God. It's a transformation that goes beyond outward actions and religious rituals. It must reach the core of our being. When our hearts are changed, we experience forgiveness, are empowered to live righteously, and become instruments of God's love in the world.

DISCUSSION QUESTIONS

1. According to Ezekiel 36:26 above, God promises to give us a new heart and spirit. What does this verse tell you about God's purposes and plan, and His role in our lives?

2. In Acts 16:14, Lydia's heart was opened by the Lord to respond to Paul's message. What does this tell you about God's initiative in changing hearts? What do you think is

our role in the process of heart transformation? Can we cooperate?

Acts 16:14 *One who heard us was a woman named Lydia, from the city of Thyatira, a seller of purple goods, who was a worshiper of God. The Lord opened her heart to pay attention to what was said by Paul.* ESV

3. Saul/Paul (Acts 9:1-19) encountered Jesus on the road to Damascus and he was radically transformed. What insights does this story provide about the power of God to change hearts?

4. Reflect on Romans 2:4, which indicates God's kindness is intended to lead us to repentance. Do you think God's kindness and grace work to change our hearts? Share examples from your life or others' experiences.

Romans 2:4 *Or do you presume on the riches of his kindness and forbearance and patience, not knowing that God's kindness is meant to lead you to repentance?* ESV

5. Discuss the parable of the prodigal son in Luke 15:11-32. How does the father's response to <u>both</u> sons reflect God's heart-changing love and forgiveness? What can we learn about repentance, forgiveness, and reconciliation in this story?

REFRESHER: **Younger son:** Demanded inheritance, squandered it, hit rock bottom, repented, returned home, was forgiven, and restored. **Older son:** Felt entitled, resentful of father's love for younger son, lacked compassion or forgiveness.

6. Consider Psalms 119:10-11 *With my whole heart I seek you; let me not wander from your commandments! 11 I have stored up your word in my heart, that I might not sin against you.* (ESV) How does hiding God's Word in our hearts contribute to heart transformation?

7. What spiritual practices or habits can help us cultivate a heart aligned with God's will?

WHAT DO I WANT TO REMEMBER?

Enter some notes and information that you want to remember about this lesson. It might be a Scripture verse or two, something new you learned, something you want to do, something you want to change, or just something you want to be sure to remember.

Wisdom to Action
Challenge

How can you open yourself more fully to God's offer of a new heart and spirit? What areas of your life need transformation through the power of the Holy Spirit?

Lesson 4
Challenging Actions Requiring The Heart

"Trust your instincts, and make judgements
on what your heart tells you.
The heart will not betray you."
David Gemmell

The Bible consistently emphasizes that actions, decisions, and attitudes should originate from a sincere and devoted heart. Delight in God should be expressed genuinely and wholeheartedly in one's relationship with God and others. In this lesson we will examine the more challenging actions required of the heart. These are the ones that might not come easily for many people.

Honesty and Truthfulness

Speaking truth and living honestly should characterize our heart actions. Ephesians 4:25 instructs us to *put off falsehood and speak truthfully* to all we come in contact with, particularly our neighbors and fellow believers. Truthfulness reflects integrity and sincerity of heart. For some this can be difficult if their core values do not reflect the standards of their faith. It becomes easy to lie when the truth will reveal your mistakes or errors in judgment.

Patience and Perseverance

Endurance and perseverance in trials should come from a steadfast heart. Patience involves trusting God's timing and purposes. These characteristics can be difficult when life is not treating you well.

Generosity

Overcoming selfishness and trusting in God's provision can sometimes be difficult, particularly if you are faced with serious financial challenges or are driven by materialistic goals. Giving and generosity should be done willingly and cheerfully, reflecting a heart that is aligned with God's heart that cares for all people regardless of their life situation. The Bible tells us that the needy will always be with us, probably to allow God to use us to provide for the needs of the disadvantaged. This allows God to reveal our greed or lack of compassion. How do you stack up?

Gratitude and Thankfulness

Expressing gratitude and thankfulness comes from a satisfied heart. Colossians 3:15 reminds us that the peace of Christ should rule in our hearts. We should be thankful for what we have, regardless if it is great or small.

Gratitude reflects a heart that recognizes God's goodness and provision. Being thankful is a consistent theme in Scripture, encouraging believers to give thanks to God for all things.

Spiritual Gifts

1 Peter 4:10 says, "*As each has received a gift, use it to serve one another, as good stewards of God's varied grace.* ESV Using our spiritual gifts for building up the kingdom can be a challenge. Many Jesus followers either don't know their gifts or don't care about them. They are reluctant to pursue their spiritual gifts because of fear, apathy, or simple rebellion.

Sincere Worship

Jesus emphasizes worshiping God in spirit and truth (John 4:23-24). Maintaining genuine devotion and participating in religious practices can be a serious battle in our spiritual journey. We are to worship with devoted hearts. If our worship is not right it can be in vain. It should reflect our wholehearted delight in God:

> **Psalms 95:6-7** *Oh come, let us worship and bow down; let us kneel before the Lord, our Maker! 7 For he is our God, and we are the people of his pasture, and the sheep of his hand.* ESV

> **John 4:23-24** *But the hour is coming, and is now here, when the true worshipers will worship the Father in spirit and truth, for the Father is seeking such people to worship him. 24 God is spirit, and those who worship him must worship in spirit and truth.* ESV

Genuine joy and worship will arise from hearts that are at peace with God. Worship is not merely an external ritual but an expression of heartfelt gratitude and sincere devotion. The delight in God must come from a heart of affection.

Humility

Proverbs teaches us that humility comes from the heart and leads to wisdom (Proverbs 22:4). Developing a humble attitude in a world that often values self-promotion and pride can be challenging. Humility before God and others must come from the heart or it will be seen as false or hypocritical. Humility requires acknowledging one's limitations and depending on God.

Praying

The power and importance of prayer is displayed in Paul's letter to the Philippians: *Do not be anxious about anything, but in everything by prayer and supplication with thanksgiving let your requests be made known to God. 7 And the peace of God, which surpasses all understanding, will guard your hearts and your minds in Christ Jesus.* (Philippians 4:6-7 ESV)

Deepening your prayer life and increasing your intimacy with God can be challenging because it requires time and intentionality. But the promise that God will guard our hearts is an awesome promise.

Summary: These characteristics are easy for some and can be very difficult for others. They may require deep introspection, reliance on God's strength and grace, or additional growth in our faith. They can be ongoing challenges for some Jesus followers.

COMMANDS THAT MAY BE EVEN MORE DIFFICULT

The actions described above can certainly be challenging, particularly if there are other forces in your life that are vying for your attention or causing you to look for solutions outside of your faith. Most of the above are recurring and you will deal with them frequently in your life. Then there are others that tend to be a bit more difficult. Why? I think the simplest explanation is that they tend to be black and white issues; there is no gray, and they demand a total commitment.

For instance, our first example below is "forgiveness." You either forgive someone or you don't. There is no partial forgiveness. The following traits will often be a significant challenge for Jesus followers. Not only are they black and white in nature, but they often require courage to practice.

Forgiveness

We are called to forgive others from the heart, just as Jesus forgives (Matthew 18:35, Colossians 3:13). Forgiving those who have deeply hurt or wronged us requires significant grace, humility, and often a fully committed relationship with Christ. Forgiving others must come from a compassionate, gracious, and obedient heart.

Purity

The Sermon on the Mount teaches us that purity of heart is essential for seeing God (Matthew 5:8). Maintaining integrity and moral purity in thoughts and actions while being bombarded with the world's values, which are usually drastically different, is a continual struggle. A pure heart involves integrity, sincerity, and a commitment to righteousness.

Repentance

Repentance results in a genuine change of heart. It literally means turning away from sin and turning towards God. In

Joel 2:12-13, the prophet urges, *Return to the Lord your God, for he is gracious and compassionate, slow to anger and abounding in love.* True repentance comes from a contrite heart that wants reconciliation with God. The heart is the place where repentance must occur.

Courage and Boldness

Courageous actions come from a brave heart. Joshua 1:9 encourages us to be strong and courageous. We are not to be afraid or discouraged, because God is with us wherever we go. Courage stems from a heart grounded in faith and trust in God. It involves taking action in the face of fear or trepidation.

Compassion and Mercy

Displaying kindness or mercy toward others flows from a compassionate, caring heart. Compassion reflects God's own heart for the vulnerable and needy.

Enduring Trials and Suffering

Endurance means finding strength and perseverance in difficult times (James 1:2-4; Romans 5:3-5). Trusting God's purposes and provision during life's trials is the result of a heart rooted in the truth of Scripture which can be difficult, particularly if you feel alone or isolated.

Eternal Perspective: Investing in Heaven

The importance of storing up treasures in heaven and living with an eternal perspective is often lost on the new or immature Christ follower. Jesus instructs believers to prioritize heavenly treasures over earthly possessions and to set their hearts on eternal rewards. (Matthew 6:19-21 and Colossians 3:1-4).

CONCLUSION

Throughout Scripture, God calls us to wholeheartedly love Him, trust Him, obey Him, and serve Him. This requires more than just outward compliance – it requires a genuine transformation of the heart. The Bible consistently teaches that genuine faith and belief are matters of the heart. It's not merely about going through the motions or following rules; it's about a deep, personal relationship with God that influences every aspect of our lives.

Throughout this lesson we have identified various challenges that will hinder our ability to live out our faith wholeheartedly. These include doubts, fears, temptations, distractions, and the struggles of daily life. Such challenges test the strength of our commitment to God.

The call to do any of the things asked with all our heart and soul require an inner self that has been changed by God's grace. Psalm 51:10 implores, "Create in me a pure heart, O God, and renew a steadfast spirit within me." This prayer acknowledges our constant need for God to work within us, shaping our hearts to reflect His character more fully.

Are we willing to allow God to search our hearts and reveal areas where we need His transformation? Are we committed to pursuing wholehearted devotion to God, even when it's challenging or uncomfortable? Our words and actions should consistently align with the love, truth, and integrity that flow from a heart surrendered to God.

Let's remember that God doesn't just want our outward obedience – He desires our hearts. As we grow in our faith journey, may we continually cultivate a heart that honors and glorifies God in everything we do. Let's encourage one another to pursue God with all our heart mind, body, and strength.

Let the words of my mouth and the meditation of
my heart be acceptable in your sight,
O Lord, my rock and my redeemer.
Psalm 19:14 ESV

DISCUSSION QUESTIONS

1. What are the obstacles or distractions that compete for your wholehearted devotion to God?

2. In what areas of your faith walk do you struggle being truthful or open with God?

3. What are some common challenges or doubts that hinder your ability to forgive?

4. Share a personal experience of receiving or extending forgiveness that would be meaningful or encouraging to the group.

5. How can we be sure our worship is sincere and pleasing to God?

6. What do you think it means "to walk humbly with your God?" (Micah 6:8)

7. What are some practical ways we can develop humility in our interactions with others?

8. How does purity of heart affect your spiritual walk and relationship with God? First Peter 1:22 says, "*Having purified your souls by your obedience to the truth for a sincere brotherly love, love one another earnestly from a pure heart.*" ESV

9. Do you think courage is important in living out our faith? Why? Share an example of a biblical character who displayed courage or boldness. What can we learn from this example?

10. How do you think showing compassion and mercy to one another reflects the heart of God?

11. Do you think trials and hardships deepen our faith and reliance on God or do they tend to weaken our relationship with Him? Can you think of one or two biblical characters that grew spiritually because they persevered through difficulties? Explain.

WHAT DO I WANT TO REMEMBER?

Enter some notes and information that you want to remember about this lesson. It might be a Scripture verse or two, something new you learned, something you want to do, something you want to change, or just something you want to be sure to remember.

Wisdom to Action
Challenge

What practical measures can you implement to better guard your heart? How will you cultivate a heart that is more aligned with God's will in the coming days?

Lesson 5
Do It With *ALL* Your Heart

"The difference between a successful person
and others is not a lack of strength,
not a lack of knowledge,
but rather a lack of will."
Vince Lombardi

INTRODUCTION

In this lesson we will look exclusively at the Scriptures that tell us to do something with ALL our heart, soul, etc. We have identified ten instructions or actions that are to be carried out with all our being versus other similar instructions that do not use the modifier "all." We believe the issue here is that these particular actions cannot be successful if we are only partially committed. It's the same as the old story about the importance of breakfast for the chicken versus the pig. The pig is fully committed!

- **SEEK** the LORD
- **LOVE** the LORD
- **SERVE** the LORD
- **OBEY** the LORD
- **RETURN** to the LORD
- **PRAISE** the LORD
- **TRUST** the LORD
- **WORK** as working for the Lord
- **REPENTANCE** from sin
- **BELIEVE** in Jesus

We are not going to differentiate between the phrases that have a different list of objects: heart, soul, mind, strength, body, etc. We will assume that there is no real difference between committing with the heart or with the heart, soul, mind, body, or strength. The focus will be on the behavior that is to be done with all our self or inner self. There is something else inherently required between doing something with your heart and doing it with <u>all</u> your heart.

Q1. What do you learn about <u>seeking God</u> with all your heart in the following passages?

Deuteronomy 4:29 *But from there you will seek the Lord your God and you will find him, if you search after him with all your heart and with all your soul.* ESV [See also Jer 29:13]

Psalms 119:2 *Blessed are they who keep his statutes and seek him with all their heart.* NIV

Q2. What do you learn about <u>loving God</u> with all your heart in the following passages?

<u>Old Testament</u>
Deut 6:4-9 *Hear, O Israel: The LORD our God, the LORD is one. 5 Love the LORD your God with all your heart and with all your soul and with all your strength. 6 These commandments that I give you today are to be upon your hearts. 7 Impress them on your children. Talk about them when you sit at home and when you walk along the road,*

when you lie down and when you get up. 8 Tie them as symbols on your hands and bind them on your foreheads. 9 Write them on the doorframes of your houses and on your gates. NIV

Deuteronomy 13:3 *The LORD your God is testing you to find out whether you love him with all your heart and with all your soul.* NIV

Deuteronomy 30:6 *The LORD your God will circumcise your hearts and the hearts of your descendants, so that you may love him with all your heart and with all your soul, and live.* NIV

New Testament
Matthew 22:37 *And he said to him, "You shall love the Lord your God with all your heart and with all your soul and with all your mind."* ESV [also Mk 12:30 and Lk 10:27]

1 Timothy 1:5 *The goal of this command is love, which comes from a pure heart and a good conscience and a sincere faith.* NIV

1 Peter 1:22 *Now that you have purified yourselves by obeying the truth so that you have sincere love for your brothers, love one another deeply, from the heart.* NIV

Q3. What do we learn about <u>serving the LORD</u> with all your heart in the following passages?

Deuteronomy 10:12-13 *And now, O Israel, what does the LORD your God ask of you but to . . . serve the LORD your God with all your heart and with all your soul, 13 and to observe the LORD's commands and decrees that I am giving you today for your own good?* NIV [See also Joshua 22:5]

Deuteronomy 11:13-15 *And if you will indeed obey my commandments that I command you today, to love the Lord your God, and to serve him with all your heart and with all your soul, 14 he will give the rain for your land . . . you may gather in your grain and your wine and your oil. 15 And he will give grass in your fields for your livestock, and you shall eat and be full.* ESV

1 Samuel 12:20, 24-25 *"Do not be afraid," Samuel replied. "You have done all this evil; yet do not turn away from the LORD, but serve the LORD with all your heart. . . . 24 But be sure to fear the LORD and serve him faithfully with all your*

heart; consider what great things he has done for you. 25 Yet if you persist in doing evil, both you and your king will be swept away." NIV

Q4. What do you learn about <u>obeying God</u> with all your heart in the following passages?

Deuteronomy 26:16 *The LORD your God commands you this day to follow these decrees and laws; carefully observe them with all your heart and with all your soul.* NIV

Deuteronomy 30:2-3 *. . . and when you and your children return to the LORD your God and obey him with all your heart and with all your soul according to everything I command you today, 3 then the LORD your God will restore your fortunes and have compassion on you and gather you again from all the nations where he scattered you.* NIV

Deuteronomy 30:17-18 *But if your heart turns away and you are not obedient, and if you are drawn away to bow down to other gods and worship them, 18 I declare to you*

this day that you will certainly be destroyed. You will not live long in the land you are crossing the Jordan to enter and possess. NIV

Proverbs 3:1-2 *My son, do not forget my teaching, but keep my commands in your heart, 2 for they will prolong your life many years and bring you prosperity.* NIV

Q5. What do you learn about <u>returning to the LORD</u> with all your heart in the following passages?

1 Samuel 7:3 *And Samuel said to the whole house of Israel, "If you are returning to the LORD with all your hearts, then rid yourselves of the foreign gods and the Ashtoreths and commit yourselves to the LORD and serve him only, and he will deliver you out of the hand of the Philistines."* NIV [See also Jeremiah 3:9-10]

Joel 2:12-13 *"Even now," declares the LORD, "return to me with all your heart, with fasting and weeping and mourning. 13 Rend your heart and not your garments. Return to the LORD your God, for he is gracious and compassionate, slow to anger and abounding in love, and he relents from sending calamity."* NIV

REPENTANCE: Repentance involves a genuine turning away from sin and returning to God with humility and contrition. Psalm 51:17 states, "The sacrifices of God are a broken spirit; a broken and contrite heart, O God, you will not despise."

Q6. What do you learn about <u>praising God</u> (worship) with all your heart in the following passages?

Psalms 138:1 I will praise you, O LORD, with all my heart; before the "gods" I will sing your praise. NIV

1 Sam 12:20-22 *"Don't be afraid," Samuel reassured them. "You have certainly done wrong, but make sure now that you <u>worship the Lord with all your heart</u>, and don't turn your back on him. 21 Don't go back to worshiping worthless idols that cannot help or rescue you—they are totally useless! 22 The Lord will not abandon his people, because that would dishonor his great name. For it has pleased the Lord to make you his very own people."* NLT

Q7. What do you learn about <u>trusting God</u> with all your heart in the following passages?

Proverbs 3:5-6 *Trust in the LORD with all your heart and lean not on your own understanding; 6 in all your ways acknowledge him, and he will make your paths straight.* NIV

Q8. What do you learn about <u>working</u> with all your heart in the following passages?

Colossians 3:23 *Whatever you do, work at it with all your heart, as working for the Lord, not for men,* NIV

Q9. What do you learn about <u>believing in God</u> with all your heart in the following passage?

Acts 8:37 *And Philip said, "If you <u>believe</u> with all your heart you may." And he replied, "I believe that Jesus Christ is the Son of God."* NKJV

WHOLEHEARTED DEVOTION – Other

There are other passages that emphasize the importance of complete devotion, sincere faith, and wholehearted commitment to God. But, they do not specifically say "with all your heart." For example, Joshua 22:5 specifies multiple actions requiring total commitment:

Only be very careful to observe the commandment and the law that Moses the servant of the Lord commanded you, to <u>love</u> the Lord your God, and to <u>walk</u> in all his ways and to <u>keep</u> his commandments and to <u>cling</u> to him and to <u>serve</u> him with all your heart and with all your soul. (Joshua 22:5 ESV)

Q10. What do we learn in the following passages about our commitment?

1 Timothy 1:5-7 *The aim of our charge is love that issues from a pure heart and a good conscience and a sincere faith. 6 Certain persons, by swerving from these, have wandered away into vain discussion, 7 desiring to be teachers of the law, without understanding either what they are saying or the things about which they make confident assertions.* ESV

Hebrews 10:22 . . . *let us draw near with a true heart in full assurance of faith, with our hearts sprinkled clean from an evil conscience and our bodies washed with pure water.* ESV

Psalm 51:16-17 *For you will not delight in sacrifice, or I would give it; you will not be pleased with a burnt offering. 17 The sacrifices of God are a broken spirit; a broken and contrite heart, O God, you will not despise.* ESV

James 4:8 *Draw near to God, and he will draw near to you. Cleanse your hands, you sinners, and purify your hearts, you double-minded.* ESV

CONCLUSION

The key to committing all of your inner being to actions that require all your heart lies in understanding the depth and completeness of commitment that is being required. We have explored ten instructions given to Jesus followers, each emphasizing the importance of engaging not just our outward actions but our entire inner selves— our hearts, minds, souls, or spirits. These instructions are vital for our journey of faith. They call for a level of dedication that goes beyond mere compliance. Frankly, they call for wholehearted devotion and surrender to God.

The distinction between doing something with your heart and doing it with all your heart lies in the depth of commitment and sincerity involved. When we seek the Lord with all our heart, we are acknowledging His lordship over every aspect of our lives – desires, decisions, and actions. Loving the Lord with all our heart means prioritizing Him above all else and letting His love permeate every relationship and interaction. Serving and obeying the Lord with all our heart requires humility, selflessness, and a willingness to submit to His authority.

God desires our wholehearted commitment in almost everything we do. He sees beyond our outward actions to the sincerity of our hearts. We must try to seek, love, serve, obey, return, praise, trust, repent, and believe with all our inner being. In so doing, we honor God and experience the fullness of His presence and blessing in our lives.

> *And you shall love the Lord your God with all your heart and with all your soul and with all your mind and with all your strength.*
> Mark 12:30 ESV

DISCUSSION QUESTIONS

1. Practically, what does it mean to you to <u>love the Lord</u> with all your heart, soul, mind, and strength?

2. How do you think <u>seeking</u> (pursuing) the Lord with <u>all</u> your heart should impact your daily life decisions and priorities?

3. What are some practical actions or disciplines that you think would help you cultivate a deeper commitment to seeking God with all your heart?

4. Why is <u>serving</u> the Lord with <u>all</u> your heart an essential aspect of Christian discipleship?

5. Share a personal experience of how serving others has deepened your faith walk.

6. How difficult is it for you to be obedient and walk in His ways? Do you think obedience to God reflects your trust and reverence for Him? What is the secret to obedience?

7. How do you personally overcome the challenges and temptations to be disobedient?

8. What does it mean to return to the Lord with all your heart after times of spiritual drift, apathy, or rebellion? What is necessary to make that return successful?

9. How would you describe the relationship between trusting the Lord with <u>all</u> your heart and experiencing His peace in times of (a) calm or (b) uncertainty?

10. Do you take the Lord with you to work? How does working for the Lord with all your heart impact your attitude towards your job, your coworkers, or your employer?

WHAT DO I WANT TO REMEMBER?

Enter some notes and information that you want to remember about this lesson. It might be a Scripture verse or two, something new you learned, something you want to do, something you want to change, or just something you want to be sure to remember.

Wisdom to Action
Challenge

In what area of your spiritual life do you need to commit more wholeheartedly? How can you demonstrate a more complete, sincere, and diligent commitment to God in this area?

Lesson 6
Encountering the Divine

"God is most glorified in us
when we are most satisfied in Him."
John Piper

WELL-KNOWN CHARACTERS

There are a number of characters in the Bible, both well-known and lesser-known, who experienced significant heart transformations upon encountering God or Jesus. The stories of these characters illustrate the transformative power of encountering God, showing how lives are changed from sinfulness, doubt, or fear to faith, obedience, and bold proclamation of God's truth. Their examples inspire and encourage us to embrace encounters with God that lead to profound spiritual growth. Note how each example provided below highlights the transformative impact of encountering the living God.

1. **Paul (formerly Saul):**

   - Encounter: Dramatic conversion on the road to Damascus (Acts 9:1-19).
   - Transformation: From a persecutor of Christians to a fervent apostle and missionary for Jesus Christ.

2. **Peter**:

   - Encounter: Multiple encounters with Jesus, including his call to discipleship (Luke 5:1-11) and restoration after denying Him (John 21:15-19).
   - Transformation: From impulsive and often fearful follower to a bold leader in the early church.

3. **Zacchaeus**:

   - Encounter: Zacchaeus climbs a tree and Jesus' visits Zacchaeus' house (Luke 19:1-10).
   - Transformation: From a greedy tax collector to a repentant and generous disciple.

4. **Nicodemus**:

   - Encounter: Nighttime conversation with Jesus about being born again (John 3:1-21) and later defending Jesus before the Pharisees (John 7:45-52; John 19:38-42).
   - Transformation: From a cautious and curious Pharisee to a believer who publicly aligned himself with Jesus.

5. **The Samaritan Woman at the Well**

   - Encounter: Conversation with Jesus at the well where He describes living water (John 4:1-42) and indicates He is the Messiah.
   - Transformation: From a woman with a checkered past to an evangelist who proclaimed Jesus as the Messiah to her community.

6. **Mary Magdalene**:

- Encounter: Jesus' deliverance from seven demons (Luke 8:2).
- Transformation: From a woman afflicted by demons to a devoted follower of Jesus who witnessed his crucifixion, burial, and resurrection.

7. **Matthew (Levi), the Tax Collector**:

- Encounter: Jesus' call to follow him (Matt 9:9-13).
- Transformation: From a despised tax collector to a disciple of Jesus and later an apostle who authored the Gospel of Matthew.

LESSER-KNOWN CHARACTERS

8. **The Demon-Possessed Man**:

- Encounter: Jesus' deliverance from demons (Mark 5:1-20).
- Transformation: From living among the tombs, and tormented by demons, to being restored to his right mind and proclaiming Jesus' works in the Decapolis.

9. **The Woman Caught in Adultery**:

- Encounter: Brought before Jesus by the scribes and Pharisees to test Him (John 8:1-11).
- Transformation: From facing condemnation to receiving forgiveness and a directive to go and sin no more, demonstrating a change in heart and perspective.

10. **The Blind Beggar (Bartimaeus):**

- **Encounter**: Healed by Jesus on the road to Jericho (Mark 10:46-52).
- **Transformation**: From blindness and societal marginalization to physical sight and a newfound faith in Jesus as the Messiah.

11. **Cornelius** (a Roman Centurion):

- Encounter: Vision and encounter with an angel directing him to send for Peter (Acts 10:1-8).
- Transformation: From a devout Gentile, seeking God but unfamiliar with Jesus, to a believer in Jesus Christ upon hearing Peter's message and receiving the Holy Spirit (Acts 10:34-48).

12. **The Philippian Jailer:**

- Encounter: Witnessed the miraculous release of Paul and Silas from prison (Acts 16:25-34).
- Transformation: From a fearful jailer to a believer in Jesus Christ, along with his entire household, baptized and demonstrating hospitality and care towards Paul and Silas.

MORE THAN AN ENCOUNTER

There are other individuals whose lives were marked by more than just an encounter with God. Their lives were changed or transformed resulting in wholehearted devotion and service to God. Their lives serve as powerful examples of what it means to prioritize and center one's entire being on loving and serving the Lord.

David
King David is often described as a man after God's own heart (1 Samuel 13:14; Acts 13:22). Despite his flaws and failures, David displayed deep love and devotion to God throughout his life, as seen in his psalms of praise, worship, repentance, and trust in God's faithfulness.

Mary (Sister of Martha and Lazarus)
Mary is known for her act of sitting at Jesus' feet and listening to his teaching, demonstrating her deep spiritual hunger and devotion (Luke 10:38-42).

Job
Job is described as a blameless and upright man who feared God and turned away from evil (Job 1:1). Despite experiencing immense suffering and loss, Job maintained his integrity and unwavering trust in God, declaring, "Though he slay me, yet will I hope in him" (Job 13:15).

Hannah
Hannah, the mother of Samuel, demonstrated profound faith and devotion in her prayer for a child (1 Samuel 1). She made a vow to dedicate her son to the Lord's service, and after Samuel's birth, she praised God with a prayer that exalted God's sovereignty and faithfulness (1 Sam 2).

Daniel
Daniel exemplified unwavering faith and commitment to God throughout his life. Despite facing persecution and threats, Daniel remained faithful in prayer and obedience to God's commands, even at the risk of his life (Daniel 6).

Abraham
Known as the father of faith, Abraham demonstrated unwavering trust and obedience to God. His willingness to obey God's command to sacrifice Isaac, his beloved son (Genesis 22), illustrated his deep faith and devotion.

Esther
Queen Esther courageously risked her life to save her people (the Jews) from genocide, following the guidance and providence of God (Book of Esther). Her willingness to step forward in faith and obedience to God's calling exemplifies her deep love for her people and trust in God's plan.

Elijah
The prophet Elijah boldly confronted idolatry in Israel and demonstrated unwavering faith in God's power. His victorious showdown against the prophets of Baal on Mount Carmel (1 Kings 18) and his encounters with God in moments of despair (1 Kings 19) reveal his deep devotion and reliance on God.

John the Baptist
John the Baptist devoted his life to preparing the way for Jesus and proclaiming the coming of the Messiah. He lived a humble and austere life, preaching repentance and baptizing people in preparation for Jesus' ministry (Matthew 3; Mark 1:1-8). He was rewarded with the privilege of announcing the arrival of Christ: "*Behold, the Lamb of God.*" (John 1:29 ESV)

COMMON TRAITS OF FULLY DEVOTED FOLLOWERS

From the examples above we can observe several common responses and characteristics or traits that reflect the individual follower's deep devotion and service to God. Following is a brief description of those characteristics.

Obedience
These individuals all demonstrated a willingness to obey God's commands and trust in His promises, even in the face of uncertainty or difficulty. They believed in God's

faithfulness and sovereignty, which motivated their obedience. For example: Abraham's willingness to sacrifice Isaac and the Virgin Mary's acceptance of God's plan for Jesus' incarnation.

Courage
Many of them exhibited courage and boldness in their faith. They were willing to take risks and stand firm in their convictions for the sake of God's kingdom. Good examples are Esther approaching the king to save her people and Elijah confronting the prophets of Baal.

Sacrificial Love
There is a recurring theme of sacrificial love among many of these individuals. They were willing to sacrifice their own comfort, desires, and sometimes even their lives for the sake of God and others. For example, Paul endured persecution and imprisonment for preaching the gospel.

Humility
Many of the followers demonstrated humility before God, recognizing their own inadequacies and relying completely on God's strength and guidance. For example, Job submitted to God's sovereignty despite his suffering and John the Baptist recognized Jesus' superiority. Mary (Martha's sister) sitting at Jesus' feet displayed her complete devotion to Him, even while her sister was annoyed with her because she was not helping with the required work.

Worship
In many cases their love for God overflowed in acts of worship and praise. They expressed their adoration and reverence for God through prayers, songs of praise, and declarations of His greatness. We see evidence of this in David's Psalms of praise and Mary's Magnificat (Luke 1:14-55)

Faithfulness

Individuals also exhibited great steadfastness in their faith, remaining faithful to God's call while enduring trials and challenges. Their love for God sustained them through difficult circumstances and empowered them to persevere. Daniel's faithfulness in prayer despite the king's opposition and Paul's perseverance in spreading the gospel are good examples.

Service

Their love for God was often demonstrated through acts of service and ministry to others. They actively participated in God's work of redemption while sharing His love and truth with those around them. Both Peter and John cared for and led the early church.

Relationship

Finally, these individuals all had intimate relationships with God. They sought communion with Him through prayer, meditation on His Word, and personal service.

These common responses highlight how wholehearted love for Jesus or God manifests itself in a variety of attitudes and actions, all rooted in a deep-seated commitment to trust and serve God with their entire being. Their lives serve as powerful examples and inspiration for believers today, encouraging us to love God wholeheartedly and live out our faith with similar devotion and passion.

CONCLUSION

In exploring the common traits of fully committed followers we uncover foundational principles that shape a life dedicated to God's purposes and glory. These characteristics are not merely ideals but essential components of a vibrant and authentic Christian life. Obedience and trust form the bedrock of a relationship with God, and they also indicate our willingness to submit to His will and guidance. Courage and sacrificial love compel us to step beyond our comfort zones, embrace the call to love others as Christ loved us, and even compel us toward acts of self-sacrifice. Humility and submission cultivate a spirit that acknowledges God's sovereignty and puts His ways above our own.

We will enthusiastically worship and praise Him through devotion and gratitude. His greatness solidifies our desire to serve Him. Faithfulness and perseverance sustain us through trials and temptations, anchoring our hope in His faithfulness. Intimacy with God is the cornerstone of our faith journey, deepening our knowledge of Him. As followers of Jesus, we are called to embody these traits:

- **In our relationships:** Practicing forgiveness, compassion, and kindness towards others.

- **In our work and vocation:** Working diligently and ethically, viewing our jobs as opportunities for service and witness.

- **In our worship:** Engaging wholeheartedly in worship and prayer, cultivating a spirit of reverence and awe.

- **In our personal growth:** Pursuing spiritual disciplines that deepen our intimacy with God and strengthen our faith.

- **In our community:** Serving others through acts of mercy, justice, and evangelism, reflecting God's love to a broken world.

By intentionally cultivating these traits, we not only honor God but also reflect His character to those around us, becoming instruments through which His light and love shine brightly.

The traits of fully committed followers of Jesus Christ are not mere attributes to strive for but transformative elements that shape us into Christ-likeness. They enable us to live out our faith authentically, impacting our world for His kingdom. As we embody these traits we continually seek to glorify God in all that we do, reflecting His grace and truth to a world in need of a Savior.

DISCUSSION QUESTIONS

1. What do you think it means to have a personal encounter with Jesus or God?

2. Reflecting on the stories of Paul (Saul), Peter, and Zacchaeus, what similarities do you see in their encounters with Jesus? How did their lives change as a result of meeting Jesus?

3. Have you ever experienced a moment where you personally felt God's presence or guidance in a significant way? How did that experience impact your life?

4. How do you think encountering Jesus differs from merely knowing about Him intellectually?

5. Discuss the transformation of the Samaritan woman at the well. What lessons can we learn from her encounter with Jesus? (John 4)

6. Reflecting on Nicodemus or the blind beggar Bartimaeus, what obstacles or preconceptions might prevent people from seeking an encounter with Jesus or God today?

7. How can encountering Jesus help us navigate the challenges, doubts, and difficult circumstances in our lives?

8. Discuss the experience of Cornelius, the Roman centurion, or the Philippian jailer. What insights do their stories provide about the inclusiveness and transformative power of God's grace?

9. How do you think a personal encounter with Jesus might impact your relationships with others, both within and outside your faith community?

10. Share examples from your life or from the lives of friends where encountering Jesus led to a change in vocation, calling, or life direction.

11. What practical steps can we take to cultivate a deeper relationship with Jesus on a daily basis, beyond just Sunday worship?

12. How do you think encountering Jesus today would challenge our cultural or societal norms, values, and priorities? Reflect on the impact of encountering Jesus today when you are in the depths of a personal crisis. How might a strong faith in God influence the outcome?

WHAT DO I WANT TO REMEMBER?

Enter some notes and information that you want to remember about this lesson. It might be a Scripture verse or two, something new you learned, something you want to do, something you want to change, or just something you want to be sure to remember.

Wisdom to Action
Challenge

Reflect on a recent encounter with God. How did it change your heart? What steps can you take to act on this transformation more boldly in your daily life?

Lesson 7
The Blind Man

"Jesus does not give recipes that show
the way to God as other teachers of
religion do. He is Himself the way."
Ravi Zacharias

NOTE: For simplicity we will refer to the blind man as
the "blind man" both before and after he is healed.

THE CONTEXT

The Gospel of John describes only eight miracles of Jesus,
called *signs*. This is the sixth sign. Prior to this healing sign
John has reported, beginning in 8:31, conversations that
Jesus was having about Abraham. Jesus said He knew the
Jews were Abraham's descendants but that they were
acting like the devil was their father, not Abraham. Jesus
further stated that if they were truly Abraham's children,
they would act like Abraham.

Jesus continued to berate the people and said they
belonged to their father, the devil, and they were not
children of God. In 8:47 He said that if they were children
of God then they would hear what God said, but because
they did not hear, then they were not His children.

The people responded by name-calling: they called him a
Samaritan and said he was demon-possessed. Jesus said

their words were nonsense and that anyone who obeyed Him would never see death. This last statement caused further consternation and they asked Him if He was greater than Abraham. Jesus aggravated the Jews even more when He said that He knew God, the Father, but they did not.

The Jews were still blinded to the truth and finally Jesus said He would tell them the truth: "before Abraham was, I am." (NIV) In effect, Jesus was claiming to be God. As a result of that statement the Jews prepared to stone Him (John 8:59), but Jesus slipped away. As He was walking along He came across a blind man.

WHAT DO WE KNOW?

John tells about several people and conversations in chapter 9. Although they all revolve around the healing of the blind man, they touch on other but related subjects. In order to better understand the different issues, I have outlined the story of the healing and its consequences under each character or group of characters in the story.

Disciples

- The disciples assumed that the man's blindness was due to either his sin or his parent's sin, a common belief of the day.
- Jesus stated that neither the blind man nor the parents had sinned.

Jesus
- Jesus told the disciples that the blindness was not due to sin.
- Jesus said the blindness occurred so God's work could be displayed in the blind man's life.

- Jesus healed the blind man. He mixed mud with saliva, put it on the blind man's eyes, and told him to wash it off in the Pool of Siloam.
- Jesus asked if the blind man believed in the Son of Man.
- Jesus told the blind man that He was the Son of Man.
- The blind man believed and worshipped Jesus.

Blind Man (from birth)
- He followed Jesus' instructions, washed off the mud, and came home with vision.
- He told his friends that Jesus healed him and described the process.
- His friends took him to the Pharisees, told them about Jesus, and claimed Jesus was a prophet.
- After talking with the parents, the Pharisees summoned the blind man and said Jesus was a sinner.
- The blind man said he knew nothing about Jesus being a sinner, but simply said, "I was blind and now I see."
- The Jews wanted to know how the blind man was healed.
- The blind man said, "I already told you. Why do you want to hear it again?"
- In response to the Pharisee's repeated demand for an explanation, the blind man asked them, "Do you want to become His disciples too?"
- The Jews got angry and said they didn't know anything about this Jesus.
- The blind man responded that it was remarkable they didn't know about Jesus, since Jesus performed a miracle and God doesn't do miracles through sinners.
- Finally, the blind man said that no one had ever done such a miracle before and if Jesus were not from God, He could do nothing, implying He must be from God.
- The Jews threw the blind man out of the synagogue (probably excommunicated him).

Pharisees/Jews
- The Pharisees asked the blind man how he was healed, and he repeated the story he had told his neighbors.
- The Pharisees again asked the blind man about Jesus because they still did not believe the story.
- The Pharisees sent for the blind man's parents.
- They asked the parents how it was possible their son could now see, if he was really born blind.
- Getting nowhere with the parents, they summoned the blind man again.
- They threatened the blind man and said they knew that Jesus was a sinner (He "worked" on the Sabbath).
- When the blind man confirmed again that he could see, they asked him how Jesus opened his eyes.
- The blind man asked the Jews why they wanted to hear again: was it because they wanted to be His disciples too?
- The Jews became very angry and began insulting the blind man.
- The Jews accused the blind man of being Jesus' disciple, and claimed they were disciples of Moses.
- The blind man asked how they knew about Moses, but they didn't know about Jesus.
- The Jews responded to the blind man's claim that Jesus must be from God because no one had ever done such a miracle, by claiming he was steeped in sin since birth.
- The Jews became so angry, they threw the blind man out of the synagogue (probably refers to some form of excommunication).

Parents of the Blind Man
- The parents verified he was their son and was born blind.
- They didn't know how he regained his sight.

- They told the Pharisees to ask their son as "he can speak for himself."
- The parents were afraid of being thrown out of the synagogue if they claimed Jesus was the Messiah.

IMPLICATIONS AND OBSERVATIONS

This chapter begins with Jesus and the disciples discussing sin. The disciples' assumption that either the blind man or his parents had sinned was the result of the prevailing thought that suffering was the result of sin. Good things happened to good people and bad things happened to bad people.

When the Pharisees tried to determine how the blind man was healed, some of them believed Jesus was a sinner because mixing the mud and putting it on the blind man's eyes constituted working on the Sabbath. The debate and doubt among the Pharisees over the healing revolved around the question of a sinner's ability to perform miraculous signs. The Pharisees wanted to believe that there was no miraculous healing even though the blind man could now see.

The dilemma for the Pharisees was that the only alternative was that Jesus had in fact performed the miracle and therefore must have been sent by God. This dilemma is very similar to the Creationist and Evolutionist debate. The evolutionist will take his theories to the grave because the only viable alternative is the existence of a Creator God.

Being experts in the Scriptures, the Pharisees should have known that giving sight to the blind was prophesied by Isaiah as an expected activity of the coming Messiah:

Isaiah 29:18 . . . *and out of their gloom and darkness the eyes of the blind shall see.* ESV
Isaiah 35:5 *Then the eyes of the blind shall be opened* . . . ESV

DISCUSSION QUESTIONS

In reading this story about the blind man it is easy to lock in on him and his encounter with Jesus. But remember, the Pharisees also encountered Jesus and their response may be even more instructive than the joy of the blind man.

1. Explain Jesus' response in John 9:3, *"Jesus answered, "It was not that this man sinned, or his parents, but that the works of God might be displayed in him."* ESV

2. In 9:17 why would the Pharisees turn again for an explanation from the blind man?
John 9:17 *So they said again to the blind man, "What do you say about him, since he has opened your eyes?" He said, "He is a prophet."* ESV

3. In 9:18, the Pharisees sent for the parents, probably to determine if the son had really been blind, or to discredit the miracle. What did the parents tell the Pharisees and why? (See 9:21)

4. In 9:24 the Pharisees said they knew the blind man was a sinner. In 9:26 they asked how his eyes were opened, and he challenged them by saying: *"I have told you already, and you would not listen. Why do you want to hear it again? Do you also want to become his disciples?"* (John 9:27 ESV) What is happening here?

5. How would you characterize the exchanges between the blind man and the Pharisees in 9:26-34?

6. The blind man responded to the insults of the Pharisees as follows:

John 9:30-33 . . . *"Why, this is an amazing thing! You do not know where he [Jesus] comes from, and yet he opened my eyes. 31 We know that God does not listen to sinners, but if anyone is a worshiper of God and does his will, God listens to him. 32 Never since the world began has it been heard that anyone opened the eyes of a man born blind. 33 If this man were not from God, he could do nothing."* ESV

What is the blind man basically saying?

7. How did the Pharisees respond to the blind man's explanation in 9:34?

John 9:34 *They answered him, "You were born in utter sin, and would you teach us?" And they cast him out.* ESV

8. How did the blind man's understanding of Jesus change during the timeframe of chapter 9? Record how the blind man referred to or felt about Jesus in each of the following verses:

9:11

9:17

9:27

9:33

9:38

9. This is a significant change! In a very short time the blind man's perception of Jesus went from seeing Him as a mere man to calling on Him as Lord. How would you explain this change of understanding?

10. What was the blind man's assertion in 9:31 and what does it mean?

John 9:31 *We know that God doesn't listen to sinners, but if anyone is God-fearing and does His will, He listens to him.*

11. In 9:34 it says that they "threw him out." What do you think this means?

12. Has anyone ever challenged your faith to the point you had to defend yourself? How did you do?

13. Have you established any position about God, Jesus, the Holy Spirit, or Scripture that is impacting your relationship with God? Is there anything in the Bible that you don't believe or don't understand? Is there anything your church claims as truth that you don't believe or don't understand?

14. The hearts of the Pharisees were never softened to the point of being able to understand the truth. Their hearts had become hardened by time and tradition. What lessons should we learn from their encounter with Jesus?

WHAT DO I WANT TO REMEMBER?

Enter some notes and information that you want to remember about this lesson. It might be a Scripture verse or two, something new you learned, something you want to do, something you want to change, or just something you want to be sure to remember.

Wisdom to Action
Challenge

How has your encounter with Jesus transformed your spiritual insight? In what ways can you stand firm and boldly defend your faith this week?

Lesson 8
Crippled Man at Lystra

SCRIPTURE

Acts 14:8-20 Paul and Barnabas at Lystra

Now at Lystra there was a man sitting who could not use his feet. He was crippled from birth and had never walked. 9 He listened to Paul speaking. And Paul, looking intently at him and seeing that he had faith to be made well, 10 said in a loud voice, "Stand upright on your feet." And he sprang up and began walking. 11 And when the crowds saw what Paul had done, they lifted up their voices, saying in Lycaonian, "The gods have come down to us in the likeness of men!" 12 Barnabas they called Zeus, and Paul, Hermes, because he was the chief speaker. 13 And the priest of Zeus, whose temple was at the entrance to the city, brought oxen and garlands to the gates and wanted to offer sacrifice with the crowds. 14 But when the apostles Barnabas and Paul heard of it, they tore their garments and rushed out into the crowd, crying out, 15 "Men, why are you doing these things? We also are men, of like nature with you, and we bring you good news, that you should turn from these vain things to a living God, who made the heaven and the earth and the sea and all that is in them. 16 In past generations he allowed all the nations to walk in their own ways. 17 Yet he did not leave himself without witness, for he did good by giving you rains from heaven and fruitful seasons, satisfying your hearts with food and gladness." 18 Even with these words they scarcely restrained the people from offering sacrifice to them.

Paul Stoned at Lystra

19 But Jews came from Antioch and Iconium, and having persuaded the crowds, they stoned Paul and dragged him out of the city, supposing that he was dead. 20 But when the disciples gathered about him, he rose up and entered the city, and on the next day he went on with Barnabas to Derbe. ESV

THE CONTEXT

Prior to arriving in Lystra, Paul and Barnabas had been in Iconium where they had experienced both success and failure. After speaking at the synagogue a great number of both Jews and Gentile Greeks had believed. But the Jews who rejected the Gospel created a firestorm of protest. Paul and Barnabas stayed on in Iconium to confront the agitators and even performed signs and wonders.

However, the people were divided. The troublemakers decided to stone Paul and Barnabas but the believers uncovered the plan and they all fled to Lystra where they healed a crippled man. It is instructive to observe that Paul's rejection in Iconium did not cause him to abandon his mission. He simply fled from those who were trying to harm him, went to the country, and continued to preach.

Upon arrival in Lystra Paul and Barnabas observed a crippled man who was lame from birth – he had never walked. The text intentionally points out that the crippled man listened to Paul as he spoke.

CONCLUSION

Despite his condition, this crippled man listened intently to Paul's preaching. Paul perceived his faith and determined he had adequate faith to be healed. Paul commanded him to stand upright and the man was miraculously healed and began walking. But the crowd did not understand what had happened. They were astonished at the miracle but thought Paul and Barnabas were Greek gods.

The people in the crowd had very little initial understanding and little discernment of the truth. This illustrates how misguided worship can result and how human misconceptions can shape actions and reactions to genuine miracles. Paul and Barnabas were so distraught that they tore their garments, rushed into the crowd, and vehemently rejected any worship or sacrifices directed toward them.

Although the heart of the crippled man was adequate, the understanding of the crowd was totally misplaced. It is critical that we direct belief and worship towards the true living God who created all things, rather than towards human beings such as excellent teachers or preachers.

It is important to note the contrast between the crowd's fickle adulation and then the harsh rejection Paul and Barnabas faced when their message was challenged by opponents from Antioch and Iconium. The people in the crowd acted more like a mob than believers of gods. But despite the opposition and violence Paul exhibited great resilience and perseverance. He miraculously got up and continued his mission with Barnabas.

Paul had a faith and belief system that resided in the heart. He believed in God's power to heal and even his own miraculous restoration. The transformative power of genuine faith was centered in Paul's heart. True belief doesn't seek personal glory or recognition but points others towards God's glory and truth.

Again, this illustrates the importance of understanding with all your heart, and should encourage our deeper reflection and understanding of words and actions that may appear miraculous.

DISCUSSION QUESTIONS

1. Why do you think the text says that Paul observed the crippled man _closely_?

2. Do you see any significance in the text "_he had faith to be made well_"?

3. Do you think this is the same distinction as general "belief" versus "saving faith"?

4. How did Paul know he had faith to be healed? What did Paul see?

5. What do you find amazing about 14:10?

6. What did the people witnessing the healing say upon seeing the miracle? Why?

7. The people credited the healing to the Greek gods, Zeus and Hermes. Do you find this surprising?

8. A Greek priest from a Greek temple outside the city arrived. What did he do?

9. What is amazing about the last part of 14:13?

10. What did Paul and Barnabas do (not what they said) when the people thought they were gods? What is the meaning or implication?

11. How did Paul and Silas describe the Greek gods?

12. How did the people respond (14:18)?

13. Then Jews from outside Lystra (from Antioch and Iconium) came and turned the crowd against Paul and Barnabas. How could outside Jews turn the local people against Paul and Barnabas so quickly?

14. How does this story challenge us to examine our own beliefs and commitments to God, especially in the face of challenges or opposition? Have you ever been seriously challenged about your faith? What happened?

15. What could have or might have happened here if Paul and Barnabas had lacked a steadfast faith and commitment.

16. What can you conclude about the need for true heart knowledge and understanding from the response of the people and the leaders?

WHAT DO I WANT TO REMEMBER?

Enter some notes and information that you want to
remember about this lesson. It might be a Scripture verse
or two, something new you learned, something you want
to do, something you want to change, or just something
you want to be sure to remember.

Wisdom to Action
Challenge

How can you use the blessings or "miracles" in your life to point
others towards God? What steps will you take to ensure you're
directing worship towards the Creator rather than the creation?

EPILOGUE
Message For People Today

You can be encouraged today because Jesus followers have an eternal destiny that cannot be shaken!

God's Unfailing Love: We see God's deep and unfailing love for all. Jesus paid the price for all who would accept Him. God's love is unconditional sacrificial, and offers forgiveness and redemption to all who come to Him (John 3:16; Romans 5:8).

Transformation: Encountering Jesus leads to personal transformation and a renewed purpose in life. God transforms individuals who have undivided devotion to His ways and a relationship with His Son Jesus (2 Corinthians 5:17; Ephesians 2:10).

Joy and Fulfillment: Jesus brings true joy, peace, and fulfillment that surpasses our earthly pleasures and pursuits. There is lasting satisfaction in Him rather than in temporary pleasures (John 10:10; Philippians 4:7).

Life Purpose: Following Jesus with all your heart produces meaningful purpose and calling in your life. Discover and use your God-given gifts and talents to serve others and advance His kingdom (Ephesians 2:10; 1 Peter 4:10).

Community: Belonging to a community of believers that supports and encourages one another in their faith journey will bring satisfaction and contentment. The value of fellowship, accountability, and growth that come from being part of a local faith community creates great satisfaction. (Hebrews 10:24-25; Acts 2:42-47).

Eternal Hope: Christians who love and serve with all their heart have the assurance of eternal life with God through faith in Christ. Following Jesus means having your sins forgiven and an eternal relationship with God in heaven for eternity (John 3:36; Romans 6:23).

Faithfulness in Adversity: God remains faithful to His followers even in times of adversity and challenge. Those who have faith and trust in God's promises persevere in this life, knowing that He is with us through every circumstance (Romans 8:28; Hebrews 13:5-6).

Invitation to Relationship: If you do not know Jesus on a personal basis, I invite you to enter into a relationship with the living Christ (Son of God and Messiah). Respond to His love and grace by repenting of sin, believing in Him as Savior and Lord, and committing to follow Him wholeheartedly (Acts 2:38; Revelation 3:20).

Appendix A
Your Minds and Thoughts

This appendix will give you an overview of what the Bible says about our minds and thoughts. This is not an exhaustive list.

MIND

God's law on our minds
Deuteronomy 11:18   *Fix these words of mine in your hearts and minds; tie them as symbols on your hands and bind them on your foreheads.* NIV
Hebrews 8:10   *This is the covenant I will make with the house of Israel after that time, declares the Lord. I will put my laws in their minds and write them on their hearts. I will be their God, and they will be my people.* NIV [see also Hebrews 10:16]

God searches and knows our minds
Psalms 7:9   *O righteous God, who searches minds and hearts, bring to an end the violence of the wicked and make the righteous secure.* NIV
Revelation 2:23   *I will strike her children dead. Then all the churches will know that I am he who searches hearts and minds, and I will repay each of you according to your deeds.* NIV

Our minds are evil
Psalms 73:7   *From their callous hearts comes iniquity; the* <u>*evil*</u> *conceits of their minds know no limits.* NIV
Colossians 1:21   *Once you were alienated from God and were enemies in your minds because of your evil behavior.* NIV
Titus 1:15   *To the pure, all things are pure, but to those who are corrupted and do not believe, nothing is pure. In fact, both their minds and consciences are corrupted.* NIV

Understanding occurs in the mind
Isaiah 44:18   *They know nothing, they understand nothing; their eyes are plastered over so they cannot see, and their minds closed so they cannot understand.* NIV
Luke 24:38, 45   *He said to them, "Why are you troubled, and why do doubts rise in your minds?" . . . 45 Then he opened their minds so they could understand the Scriptures.* NIV
Romans 16:18   *For such people are not serving our Lord Christ, but their own appetites. By smooth talk and flattery they deceive the minds of naive people.* NIV

Our minds can be deluded
2 Corinthians 11:3   *But I am afraid that just as Eve was deceived by the serpent's cunning, your minds may somehow be led astray from your sincere and pure devotion to Christ.* NIV

Instruction: Set your minds on spiritual things
Romans 8:5   *Those who live according to the sinful nature have their minds set on what that nature desires; but those who live in accordance with the Spirit have their minds set on what the Spirit desires.* NIV
Colossians 3:2   *Set your minds on things above, not on earthly things.* NIV

Warning: Guard your minds
Philippians 4:7   *And the peace of God, which transcends all understanding, will* <u>*guard*</u> *your hearts and your minds in Christ Jesus.* NIV
1 Peter 1:13   *Therefore, prepare your minds for action; be self-controlled; set your hope fully on the grace to be given you when Jesus Christ is revealed.* NIV

Danger
Psalms 64:6   *They plot injustice and say, "We have devised a perfect plan!" Surely the mind and heart of man are cunning.* NIV
Isaiah 32:6   *For the fool speaks folly, his mind is busy with evil: He practices ungodliness and spreads error concerning the LORD; the hungry he leaves empty and from the thirsty he withholds water.* NIV

Ezekiel 38:10   *This is what the Sovereign LORD says: On that day thoughts will come into your mind and you will devise an evil scheme.* NIV

Romans 1:28   *Furthermore, since they did not think it worthwhile to retain the knowledge of God, he gave them over to a depraved mind, to do what ought not to be done.* NIV

Philippians 3:19   *Their destiny is destruction, their god is their stomach, and their glory is in their shame. Their mind is on earthly things.* NIV

Set your mind for understanding

Daniel 10:12   *Then he continued, "Do not be afraid, Daniel. Since the first day that you set your mind to gain understanding and to humble yourself before your God, your words were heard, and I have come in response to them."* NIV

Unity

Acts 4:32   *All the believers were one in heart and mind. No one claimed that any of his possessions was his own, but they shared everything they had.* NIV

1 Corinthians 1:10   *I appeal to you, brothers, in the name of our Lord Jesus Christ, that all of you agree with one another so that there may be no divisions among you and that you may be perfectly united in mind and thought.* NIV

2 Corinthians 13:11   *Finally, brothers, good-by. Aim for perfection, listen to my appeal, be of one mind, live in peace. And the God of love and peace will be with you.* NIV

Best advice

Romans 12:2   *Do not conform any longer to the pattern of this world, but be transformed by the renewing of your mind. Then you will be able to test and approve what God's will is-his good, pleasing and perfect will.* NIV

Believers have the mind of Christ

1 Corinthians 2:16   *For who has known the mind of the Lord that he may instruct him?" But we have the mind of Christ.* NIV

THOUGHTS

Man's thoughts are evil
Genesis 6:5 *The LORD saw how great man's wickedness on the earth had become, and that every inclination of the thoughts of his heart was only evil all the time.* NIV
James 2:4 *. . . have you not discriminated among yourselves and become judges with evil thoughts?* NIV

God knows and tests the thoughts of man
Psalms 94:11 *The LORD knows the thoughts of man; he knows that they are futile.* NIV
Luke 9:47 *Jesus, knowing their thoughts, took a little child and had him stand beside him.* NIV

God detests the thoughts of the wicked
Proverbs 15:26 *The LORD detests the thoughts of the wicked, but those of the pure are pleasing to him.* NIV

Fix your thoughts on God, heaven, and spiritual things
Hebrews 3:1 *Therefore, holy brothers, who share in the heavenly calling, fix your thoughts on Jesus . . .* NIV

Give thought to your ways
Proverbs 14:8 *The wisdom of the prudent is to give thought to their ways, but the folly of fools is deception.* NIV

The Word judges our thoughts
Hebrews 4:12 *For the word of God is living and active. Sharper than any double-edged sword, it penetrates even to dividing soul and spirit, joints and marrow; it judges the thoughts and attitudes of the heart.* NIV

Take captive your thoughts
2 Corinthians 10:5 *We demolish arguments and every pretension that sets itself up against the knowledge of God, and we take captive every thought to make it obedient to Christ.* NIV

WHAT DO I WANT TO REMEMBER?

Enter some notes and information that you want to remember about your mind/thoughts. It might be a Scripture verse or two, something new you learned, something you want to do, something you want to change, or just something you want to be sure to remember.

Wisdom to Action
Challenge

What negative thought patterns do you need to address? How will you actively align your thoughts with God's truth this week?

Appendix B
How To Change Your Heart

"Life can be simple and beautiful.
Focus on the good things."
Maxime Lagacé

HOW TO CHANGE YOUR HEART: Filter and control what you think, see, hear, and touch because they will influence your heart, which in turn influences your decisions.

The Senses

Our senses are the gateway to gaining knowledge, understanding, and ultimately wisdom. Such information can be both positive and negative depending on the source of the information we are receiving. For example, if all we ever listen to is classical music, we will ultimately become very knowledgeable about the writers and performers and we may even choose to learn to play an instrument because we love the music. The music has touched our heart and we not only want to listen, but we also want to participate.

If we live in a home where one or more of the parents are abusive, that abusive behavior becomes the natural order of life. We grow up in an environment where abuse (physical, mental, or emotional) is the norm and we may mimic such behavior in our own lives.

What we hear, see, and touch will have a great influence on our thinking and behaviors. If we are constantly listening to music that is vulgar, violent, or sexually explicit, that message creeps into our hearts and becomes acceptable because our minds and hearts have been conditioned to live out what our senses experience.

Consider the young boy or girl who is a tennis pro at age 16. How did they become so good at playing tennis? They probably have some natural physical talent but in addition, the one thing that these athletes have in common is they spent hours and hours on the tennis court – every day. They ate, drank, and slept tennis. Tiger Woods didn't become a great golfer because he had a natural swing. He is a great golfer because his dad had him playing golf every waking minute.

I say all this to help you understand that what you experience (think, see, hear, touch) will have a great influence on your life. That influence can be life-changing if you spend enough time in any given activity. What we are doing and what our senses are experiencing will influence our lives and that influence can be good or bad. When that influence reaches the heart and saturates our inner being we have established or created a core value that will dictate actions and decisions. Thus, it is fundamentally important to arrange your life so that your experiences influence your heart in the right manner.

The Heart

We have already adequately discussed the nature and characteristics of the "heart" in the foregoing pages. We will not repeat it here.

The Mind

In order for something to be written on the heart it has to be filtered through the mind. I must go through the process of convincing my intellect that something is true or desirable so that my heart will allow me to act on that concept, information, or principle. It will not be enough to say I believe something to be true, but that I have accepted that truth and I am committed to implementing it in my life.

You may want to pause and think about the following five questions for a minute:

1. What are your eyes and ears seeing and hearing these days? What are they used to absorbing?

2. What or who are you listening to that is influencing your actions?

3. What are you seeing that is implanting impressions on your mind and ultimately your heart?

4. What are you touching (where are you going) that is establishing your value system?

5. How are all these inputs to your heart and mind influencing your behavior?

Many of us think that a little harmless seeing and listening won't really have any impact on our lives, but that has proven not to be the case.

The heart ultimately determines our decisions and direction. But the mind is a powerful filter that impacts what our hearts will consider. Since we may want to change some fundamental characteristics in our life, we will need new information and understanding to reach the heart. But our minds must allow us to do that. If we want to change our hearts we need to condition our minds or use our minds to prepare our hearts for new input. It will be difficult to change our lives if our minds remain rigid and stubborn.

We need to stretch or open our minds to new thoughts and new ideas as well as close them to evil or useless information. What we think about will ultimately be who or what we are. If our thoughts are constantly about money and wealth our actions will soon reflect those thoughts because our hearts have been saturated with thoughts about riches, expensive cars, or big houses.

On the other hand, if we want to change our lifestyle and we begin filling our minds with information and knowledge about positive behavior, the heart will receive the message and change, even transform. But that change will not likely occur unless the input from our senses is filtered in the mind and appropriately impacts the heart producing a revised set of standards or desires.

Thus, we must be _intentional_. I must decide I want to change and then be intentional about filling the pipeline to my heart with information and knowledge that will transform my heart such that I can easily make the right choices.

The Power of Thought

I can remember my Dad saying to me on several occasions, "God gave you a brain. Use it!" Thinking seems to be a lost art these days! Many problems would disappear if we would take time to think. Not every answer has to be determined immediately. I have a motto I live by in these situations. If you insist on my answer right now, the answer is, "No."

If you are being challenged with an important issue or question, you need to produce the right answer. Thinking about important issues and questions is what successful people do. There are few decisions that can't wait at least 24 hours. I was gifted with a somewhat suspicious nature, so if you approach me with some new idea, or some fantastic opportunity, my response is likely to be, "Prove it." That pause often saves me from making mistakes. Thinking a problem through in order to understand all the ramifications leads to better solutions.

Even friends can lead us down a path we don't want to travel. Other people do not necessarily have our best interests in mind. They have their own agenda and are often looking for companions to accompany them. Unfortunately the reason they may want company is because they need it to validate their own poor judgment.

Since my thoughts are dramatically impacted by what I see, what I hear, and where I go, I need to filter those decisions to see, hear, and go based on my own core values, goals, and standards. I remember reading the question, "If all you ever listened to for ten years was country music, what would you believe?" I wasn't really sure what the author was getting at until I read his answer:

1. Everyone drinks beer and is rowdy on Saturday night.
2. Everyone owns a dog who is their best friend.
3. Everyone drives a pick-up truck.

That's funny, right? Well, it may be funny but it's also true. We become what we do. We establish values and opinions based on what we hear, see, and touch. All the techies in the reading audience have been waiting to read their favorite computer example: GIGO (Garbage In – Garbage Out). And, it's true. If you put information in your computer that is wrong, misleading, or ill-advised, (garbage), then that's what will come out as answers to your questions. The computer can only produces answers based on what it has been fed.

We are the same way. If we feed our minds and hearts garbage, then that's what we are going to get back. A life based on garbage is not very pleasant.

Fix Your Mind on What is True

Fix your mind on what is good, true, and wholesome. A changed heart can transform your life, but only if it is not fed garbage. So, give thought to what you are doing! Focus your attention on things that are uplifting and true, on subjects that uplift and do not tear down.

The fool will believe anything. He does not give thought to his ways. "Giving thought to our ways" seems like a simple solution. But that simple truth is dependent on taking the action that your thought produces. Being intentional! If we give thought to our ways we can determine the best course of action, particularly if we have taken some time to think about it.

My first question in any situation where a significant decision must be made is, "What are the alternatives?" If you don't consider any alternatives and their potential impact, your first thoughts generally seem right. Decisions made in haste often fail miserably when compared with other possible alternatives.

If you are faced with a question you have already thought about, you probably have several possible answers in mind because you already know how you want to respond in such situations. For example, I have already thought through the question of whether I will give a female co-worker a ride home alone because she is stranded. It doesn't really make any difference that I will be going right by her apartment. I'll put her in a cab and send her home – I'm not going to violate one of my core values. I can produce this response because I have thought about the situation and the alternatives in advance.

Think about the challenges to your core values. Think about the possible temptations that would cause you to violate your values. What will you do when these challenges and temptations occur? If you have already considered these challenges and thought about your response, the answers are easy. That's why core values are so valuable. They require you to think in advance about what is important to you.

For example, if you choose honesty, integrity, and truth, your life becomes much simpler when you are faced with issues, requests, or demands that tempt you to do things that would violate the law, your friend's privacy, or your own core values.

What Should You Do?

How are you going to harness the heart and mind to produce the results you desire? What must you do? What are the practical actions you can take to control what you see? How do you establish limits on what you hear? What should you avoid?

First you have to want to make changes in your life. Then, you must intentionally take some kind of action that will either limit your exposure to negative input, or open up the possibility for new, improved, and positive experiences that will begin transforming your heart.

REALITY CHECK! You may be thinking that it sounds like a lot of work and effort to make these changes in your life. Maybe! It really depends on your starting point. If you are struggling with the need to change bad behavior or bad habits it may take significant time and effort. But what is the alternative?

People who seem to have their act together have been practicing these activities for many years and it may be second nature to them. If you struggle with some of the commitments you have made, it will require effort. The first step is this: Just get started.

Decision #1: I will filter what I see.

First, take one step at a time. Most of us are not prepared to make drastic changes that impact a major part of our lives. Where is your negative input coming from? What are you reading? What are you watching on TV, the Internet, or your phone? Tackle the big and serious bad habits first. Do it with a passion. If your problem is the TV, turn it off. If you can't just do that, cancel the service.

That may sound drastic, but drastic action may be needed!

You will be amazed how quickly you can adapt to a TV-free environment. You can change and make new habits by practicing them for 30 days. If the political noise between the Republicans and Democrats is causing you to be angry all the time, stop watching the talking heads who are only performing so that you will watch the commercials. Have you ever thought about that? News is no longer news. News has become a channel to change your way of thinking.

What are you reading? If you are reading trash, your mind is full of trash and just like our oceans it will eventually cough up all the discarded trash onto the beach. If that beach is in your boss' office or in the presence of your best friend, the results may not be what you desire.

The secret of success is to focus on what you want to change or transform. If your eyes are roaming all around trying to see every little thing, change your perspective. Put limitations on certain activities and focus your attention on what you want to change. Choose one activity at a time and face it down until it is under control and then go to the next. Once you are successful with getting one questionable activity under control, it is much easier to tackle the next.

Filter what you see!

Decision #2: I will filter what I hear.

Who or what are you listening to? I stopped listening to talk shows that want to get me all excited about some topic. I realized some time ago it wasn't good for my mental health. I also realized I couldn't trust the truthfulness of what was being said. Everything seemed to be slanted to influence me toward some position that they, the programmers, wanted to promote.

So, I stopped. After a short time I didn't miss it at all because I found other things I wanted to hear, read, or visit. TV, radio, and podcasts can both encourage or poison our minds. They can bring calm or cause stress and anxiety. They can drive you crazy and take over your mind. But if you choose what you hear with forethought, the listening can be uplifting, educational, or soothing.

The music we listen to will often influence us more than we think. Young people are particularly impacted by music. Have you ever listened to the actual words of some of the edgy music these days? People who think they have to speak in vulgarities, sexually explicit language, or other shocking ways are not the people I want to listen to or people I want my children to hear.

These people are not simply expressing their free thought and right to speak openly – they are damaging everyone who listens. Sadly, they don't really care because they are chasing the almighty dollar. They want attention and shocking, explicit language is their hook.

Unfortunately that hook pierces my veil of decency and I reject their attempt to poison my mind and heart. You must do the same. Our goal has to be to control and filter the voices of evil, discord, and rebellion in order to feed our hearts and minds information that is uplifting.

So if you are among those who need help in this area of your life, consider yourself challenged. If this is not a particular problem for you, feel blessed. You may have a friend who needs your advice in this area of their life.

Filter what you hear!

Decision #3: I will filter where I go.

I will avoid places that cause me difficulty or create negative temptations. If I am married, I will never be alone with a person of the opposite sex who is not my spouse. If I am an alcoholic I will not go to bars. If I have a gambling problem, I will not go to casinos. If I have an addiction problem, I will not hang out where that addiction can be fed. If I have an eating problem, I will not go to "All you can eat" establishments. It is not that difficult to draw the line. The problem is in choosing to cross that line or choosing not to cross it!

It is very easy to identify those places that will cause us temptation. I simply make the decision to avoid those places. It's like after a breakup with a longtime boyfriend or girlfriend – I don't go to the places I know they are likely to be because I don't want to see them or talk to them.

On the positive side I will go to places that will encourage me, support me, and give me peace. The first and most natural place for many of us is our family. I need to make family a priority or life becomes a constant source of stress and conflict. I need to go places where I will grow spiritually, intellectually, and emotionally. I need to go where the activity produces joy and satisfaction, not temptation.

One of the biggest temptations may be with our friends who have other agendas. Don't be persuaded to get off the narrow path by friends or acquaintances who don't really understand your mindset. Sometimes it might be necessary to give up old friends and make new ones.

Filter where you go!

Decision 4: I will filter what I say.

Many of us are very careless about our speech and the impact it has on other people. Some even think that they can say anything they wish simply because it is their right.

Gracious speech is polite and shows respect to the one we are talking to. It is pleasing, acceptable, not grating, harsh, or vulgar. It has some lasting value and is appropriate for the situation.

The one who speaks too soon or speaks without thinking is worse than a fool. This is a serious warning to those who speak up and then think later. Speaking quickly means that our words may have little thought behind them. The result can be embarrassing and in retrospect should have been left unsaid.

Thinking before you speak can be a lifesaver. Obviously you want to have something worthwhile to contribute and pausing to speak can often produce a good result. What you don't want to do is say something hurtful or off-putting. Your comments should be helpful, useful, and on target.

It is always wise to consider if what you are saying is adding to the conversation, or just noise. Are your words worthwhile or are they just meaningless comments. Have you listened long enough that you understand the discussion? Is what you want to say actually worth saying? Is it just repeating or rehashing what someone else has said?

Under no circumstance should you lie, embellish, or shade what you are saying. Do not speak slander. Your words can have gigantic negative impact. With technology today your words can go around the world in seconds and impact people you don't know and will never meet. Your words can start fires or put them out.

Choose your words carefully.

DISCIPLINE

The key to being intentional is *self-discipline*. It is like the cross-country runner or marathoner who is training to run a race. He or she needs to be disciplined enough to practice running. The practice isn't just once in a while. It's every day! The runner needs to build up stamina and muscle tone. He needs to make his body know what to expect and be ready to run the race, hit the exhaustion wall, and continue running. Control is gained by enforcing obedience to an order or regimen. The runner wants to have an orderly or prescribed response when times get tough during the race. Self-control is essential.

128

This is true for us as well. We need to be disciplined about where we go, what we see, and what we hear. We need to be sharp mentally and emotionally. We must make daily decisions that will put us in the places so that what we see, what we hear, and where we go will have positive influences on our lives and character. If this is particularly difficult for you, find a trusted friend to hold you accountable. Give the friend permission to challenge you as well as encourage you. Then agree you will not lie to your friend about your activities.

My heart will be impacted by
what I see,
what I hear, and
where I go!

Wisdom to Action
Challenge

What specific actions will you take this week to guard your heart more effectively? How can you approach God with a more sincere heart and clearer conscience?

Transformation Road Map

Primary Takeaways

1: The heart is central to our relationship with God. It is not just the seat of emotions but the core of our being where faith lives and decisions are made.

2: Genuine faith requires a wholehearted commitment to follow Christ. We must engage our entire being – heart, soul, mind, and spirit – integrating our faith into every aspect of our lives.

3: The "heart" is the wellspring of our actions and motivations necessitating careful guarding and cultivation to ensure it aligns with God's truth.

4: God not only knows and tests our hearts, but He also offers a new heart and spirit to enable us to know Him, obey His commands, and live in a transformed relationship with Him.

5: The heart is the central command center of our being, influencing our intellect and moral choices. It is the source of our love, obedience, and relationship with Him.

6: For a Christian, doing something "with all our heart" signifies a complete, sincere, and diligent commitment to God in every aspect of life. Our heart must be aligned with God's will if our lives are to be truly pleasing to Him.

7: Encountering the Divine leads to transformative changes of the heart, turning individuals from sin, doubt, or fear toward faith, obedience, and the bold proclamation of God's truth.

8: Encountering Jesus brings not only physical healing but also spiritual insight and transformation, leading to a bold faith and willingness to defend the truth of Jesus even in the face of opposition.

9: Genuine faith directs worship and belief toward Christ. We need discernment to intentionally align our thoughts with God's truth, taking every thought captive to Christ.

10: We are required to love God with all our heart, believe in Him sincerely, and approach Him with a guilt-free conscience. Therefore, we must actively guard their hearts recognizing that it is the core of our being and the key to a valid and acceptable relationship with Him.

What are you being called to do next?

Leader Guide

This Guide is designed to give a leader answers and additional information to effectively lead a discussion of each lesson in this book.

Tips For Leading

We recommend that you begin a group discussion by reading an appropriate Scripture. It may be one that you will cover in the material or another related passage you have chosen. This will do several things:

- Allow time for everyone to get settled.
- Remind everyone of the subject and bring their minds to a common focus.
- Provide a transition from the previous activity.

Additional ice-breakers are usually not necessary, but if your group is new or members don't know each other well, you could have someone give their testimony/story at the beginning of each week. If you sense that the group needs additional focus before you begin with the discussion, conduct a short discussion about the themes of the lesson or ask about the meaning of a particular term associated with the lesson.

Goals

The discussion should center around the questions in the lesson. But remember that each person in your group has different goals and is at a different place in his or her Christian walk. Jesus may be an old friend to some but a new acquaintance to others. The dynamic of the group will vary depending on the nature of the participants.

Your goal as the Leader should be to foster understanding and familiarity with Scripture. For new believers or participants who are not comfortable with the Bible, your goal should be to help them get over that hurdle and begin to seek knowledge and understanding from His Word.

More mature participants will probably dig deeper to find personal meaning and understanding. They may particularly desire to discuss application questions and issues.

Prayer

Unless you have an outstanding person of prayer in your group, you as the leader should wrap up your discussion time with prayer that specifically reflects the discussion and the themes, purpose, and focus of the lesson.

Answers

Lesson 1 Wholehearted Commitment

Q1.
Romans 7:22
The heart (or inner being) should be delighted in God's Word.
Ephesians 3:16
Our inner being (heart) can be strengthened with His power. LEADER: Ask your group what they think this means. Ans: If the strength does not reside in the heart it will likely fail.
1 Peter 3:4
Our hearts (inner self) is of great value to God and the Bible describes our inner self as being of "unfading beauty."
Psalms 51:6 and **Psalms 139:13**
(1) God teaches us that wisdom resides in our heart (inner parts). (2) Since God is truth, He will teach us truth. (3) Ps 139 says that God created and formed our "inward parts" (heart): He created us in this manner intentionally.
Q2.
Deuteronomy 4:29 If we seek him with all our heart and soul, we will find Him.
2 Chronicles 15:12 Seeking and finding is important to God (there was a covenant). The people were to do it with all their heart and soul.
Q3.
Deuteronomy 6:5
We are to love God, not only with all our heart and soul, but all our strength.
Deuteronomy 13:3
God may test us to determine if we love Him with all our heart and soul!
Matthew 22:37
Jesus confirms the need to love with all our heart and soul and adds the requirement of "mind."
Q4.
Moses instructions also included the requirement to serve God with all our hearts and soul.
Q5.
Deuteronomy 26:16

It should not be surprising that the Lord would expect obedience and obeying His laws with all our heart and soul. See also Dt 30:2.

2 Kings 23:3
God expects all His commands, regulations, requests, and decrees to be done with all our hearts and soul.

Q6.
Turning to the Lord (repentance) must be done with all our heart and soul. It cannot be superficial.

Q7.

Psalms 19:7
God's Word and law will revive the soul.

Psalms 62:1
My soul finds rest and strength in God alone.

1 Peter 2:11
Sinful desires war against the soul (heart).

Ps 130:5-6
Our soul "waits" in hopeful anticipation for the Lord.

Proverbs 22:5
Guarding your soul (heart) will protect you from wickedness.

Q8

Colossians 4:8
The Holy Spirit (God) will encourage our hearts.

1 Thessalonians 3:13
Strengthen our hearts.

2 Thessalonians 2:16-17
Comfort our hearts and "establish" them to do good works.

2 Thessalonians 3:5
Help us find our way to God and His love.

Q9.

Matthew 10:28-31
He will also encourage us if we are persecuted.

2 Corinthians 1:3-4
God is a God of comfort. He will encourage us in our trials and suffering.

Lesson 2 The Importance and Problems of the Heart
Q1.

Jeremiah 4:4
The prophet is saying that our hearts must be circumcised.

The instruction to "circumcise your hearts" is a metaphorical expression that refers to a deep inner change. When applied to the heart, circumcision would mean the removal of anything that hinders a complete commitment to God. It's a symbolic cutting away of things like sin, hard hearts, impure motives – anything that would hinder the right relationship between God and man. The purpose is to become more receptive to God and His purposes. [See also Dt 10:16] Remember that it is a continuous process, not a one-time event. As we grow in our faith, we should continually remove anything that hinders our relationship with God. It's not about achieving perfection but about a sincere desire and ongoing effort to be closer to God.

Ezekiel 33:31
The heart is the gauge of true feelings or positions, not words that may be disguised to deceive.
Malachi 4:6
The love of family (spouse and children) comes from the heart, not the mind.
Psalms 14:1
One demonstrates he is a fool in his heart.
Psalms 26:2
If God is going to test us, He will test or examine our hearts and minds because that is what truly defines man.
Psalms 37:4
The real desires of man come from his heart.
Proverbs 11:20
Here Scripture is saying that it is the heart that makes the choices and decisions that cause God to detest the wickedness of man. In comparison He loves the "blameless" ways of men.
Q10.
Mark 7:21
Evil comes from the heart of men.
James 3:14
Hearts harbor bitter envy and selfish ambition.
Mt 15:19-20
It is not the lack of following the ceremonial rules of worship that made the people unclean, it was sin.
Q11.
It doesn't really matter what we think about God hardening hearts. We have no basis to suggest what is right, fair, just, or appropriate because we have no knowledge of the plans of God. God is sovereign meaning He can determine and do whatever He determines is needed or right. Our human hearts and minds cannot truly understand the wisdom of God.

DISCUSSION QUESTIONS
1.
The "heart" represents the core of our being where our desires, thoughts, and emotions reside. It's the seat or core of our spiritual life and the place where we make decisions that impact our relationship with God and others. The heart is crucial in shaping our faith, guiding our actions, and determining our spiritual health.
2.
The same explanation might resonate to some extent, however, assuming they do not share the Christian worldview, the spiritual dimensions tied to the heart (like sin and redemption) may not connect. They are likely to interpret "heart" more as emotions or personal inclinations rather than as a spiritual battleground or source of alignment with God's will.
3.
Proverbs 4:23 highlights the importance of guarding our hearts because it

influences <u>every</u> aspect of our lives. Our thoughts, attitudes, and actions begin with the condition of our hearts. It shapes our character, impacts our relationships, and determines our spiritual direction.

4.

Monitor the Input: Be selective about what we expose ourselves to (media, relationships; thoughts). **Implement Spiritual Habits:** Engage in practices that nurture spiritual growth (prayer, Scripture reading, fellowship). **Check Your Motives:** Regularly examine your intentions and attitudes behind your actions. **Seek Accountability:** Surround ourselves with people who can help us stay accountable in guarding our hearts.

5.

Jeremiah 17:9-10 states that the heart is deceitful above all things and desperately sick. This doesn't mean the heart is inherently evil in an irredeemable sense, but rather it describes man's tendency toward sin and the resulting need for God's transformative work.

6.

Serving God with sincerity means doing so genuinely, without hypocrisy, and with no ulterior motives. It involves wholehearted devotion, where our actions align with our core beliefs and values. We develop sincerity by maintaining transparency before God, having purity of motives, and allowing the Holy Spirit to guide and purify our hearts.

7.

A pure and devoted heart enables us to authentically worship God, fostering a genuine relationship with Him. Conversely, a distracted or hardened heart can hinder our worship experience, distancing us from God's presence.

8.

What we speak reflects what resides in our hearts (good and evil). Our words can expose areas needing spiritual growth and serve as a gauge of our spiritual health. Therefore, being mindful of our speech and seeking to align it with God's truth and love is crucial in maintaining a healthy heart before God and others.

Lesson 3 God Can Change Your Heart

Q1.

Matthew 6:19-21

In these verses, Jesus teaches about the connection between our treasures and our hearts. He emphasizes that where our treasure is, there our heart will be also, suggesting that a change in our priorities and values can lead to a transformation of the heart.

Jeremiah 31:33

This passage speaks of a new covenant in which God promises to write His law on the hearts of His people. It suggests that a change of heart is necessary for a deeper relationship with God and obedience to His commands.

Q2.
Only God knows the hearts of men! See also 2 Chronicles 6:30.
Q3.
The mind! What man is thinking! See also Jeremiah 20:12.
Q4.
God is using the heart of man to evaluate and test him.
Q5.
God's values are not man's values. Man's values are detestable to God!
LEADER: You might ask your group what they think it means that the values of men are detestable to God. Ans: There is a _big_ gap between the values of God and the values of man.
Q6.
God gave us the Holy Spirit. This is also confirmed in Romans 8:27 NIV where it says, "*And he who searches our hearts knows the mind of the Spirit, because the Spirit intercedes for the saints in accordance with God's will.*" It tells us that the Holy Spirit intercedes for men.
Q7.
We will be judged on our deeds by God who has searched our hearts and minds for motives, intent, and truth.
Q8.
God wanted a people that would love, obey and trust Him. A people that would carry out His will. He wanted a people that would take His message of love and redemption to the world. God knew all along that Israel would fail and the Gentiles would be grafted in. Israel failed because man is not capable of following God's laws.
Q9.
2 Chronicles 32:31
We know from 32:25 that Hezekiah's heart was proud and the Lord's wrath was on him, but he repented (32:26). God was clearly testing him to demonstrate Hezekiah's true heart.
Psalms 26:2
David had sinned and had repented and was asking God to test him.
James 1:2-4
Testing can occur through trials to produces character or steadfastness.
Revelation 2:23
Believers will be tested on their works, both good and bad (Matthew 16:27 and Romans 2:6).
Q10.
1 Samuel 10:9 God can supernaturally change our hearts.
Jeremiah 24:7 Man is given a heart that will recognize God.
Ezekiel 36:26 God has given us a heart and spirit that will overcome our sinful nature. We can know God.
Deuteronomy 30:6 God has circumcised our hearts and the hearts of our family – purified us for meeting Him.

DISCUSSION QUESTIONS
1.
This verse reveals God's deep desire and plan to transform our hearts and spirits. It shows that God takes an active role in our lives. His promise demonstrates His intention to renew and restore us, replacing our hardened,

unresponsive hearts with a soul that is responsive to Him. We cannot achieve this on our own but it is a gift from God, demonstrating His sovereignty and His desire for a restored relationship with us.

2.

Lydia's experience demonstrates God's desire and initiative in opening hearts to respond to His message. It emphasizes that heart transformation is ultimately the work of God. Our role in this process involves openness and willingness to receive God's Word and respond to His prompting. We can cooperate by seeking God earnestly, being receptive to His Spirit, and aligning our will with His.

3.

Saul's encounter demonstrates the radical power of God to change hearts. Saul was a persecutor of Christians, yet God's intervention completely transformed him into one of the most influential apostles of the early Christian church. This story reveals that God's power can break the hardest of hearts, leading to repentance, faith, and a life devoted to God's purposes. No one is beyond the reach of God's grace. He can and does radically change lives for His glory.

4.

Romans 2:4 emphasizes that God's kindness and grace are intended to lead us to repentance. This kindness includes God's patience, mercy, and provision despite our shortcomings. God's acts of kindness can soften our hearts and draw us closer to Him.

5.

The father's response to both sons reflects God's heart-changing love and forgiveness. The father eagerly welcomes back the repentant younger son with open arms, showing unconditional love and forgiveness. Similarly, he extends grace to the older son, inviting him to celebrate and reconcile. This parable teaches us about the depth of God's forgiveness and His desire for repentance and reconciliation.

6.

Psalm 119:10-11 emphasizes the importance of storing up God's Word in our hearts in order to guard against sin. Hiding God's Word in our hearts means internalizing Scripture, meditating on its truths, and applying it to our lives. This can renew our minds and shape our desires to live in according with God's will.

7.

Prayer and Meditation: Regularly communing with God through prayer and reflecting on His Word. **Learning:** Growing in knowledge of God's Word and applying it to daily life. **Fellowship:** Engaging in community with other believers for encouragement and accountability. **Worship:** Expressing reverence and gratitude to God through worship and praise. **Service:** Serving others selflessly, following Jesus' example of love and humility. **Obedience:** Willingly surrendering our desires and obeying God's commands. **Repentance:** Acknowledging and turning away from sin, seeking God's forgiveness.

Lesson 4 Challenging Actions Requiring The Heart
DISCUSSION QUESTIONS:

1.
Busyness: The demands of life, work, and responsibilities can crowd out intentional time with God. **Worldly Pursuits:** Materialism, worldly ambitions, and the pursuit of business or career success can overshadow prioritizing God. **Sin:** Unresolved sin or recurring temptations that draw focus away from God. **Lack of Commitment:** Not making intentional efforts to cultivate spiritual disciplines like prayer, Bible study, and fellowship. **Apathy:** Just plain laziness.

2.
Sin: Being honest about areas of disobedience, rebellion, weakness, or temptation. **Personal Struggles:** Admitting doubts, fears, or struggles with your faith. **Emotional Honesty:** Expressing true feelings, emotions, and concerns in prayer. Trusting Christian friends. **Control:** Holding back certain areas of life from God's control or guidance.

3.
Hurt and Betrayal: Deep wounds or repeated offenses that are difficult to forgive. **Resentment:** Feeling justified in holding onto anger or bitterness. **Vulnerability:** Apprehension about being hurt again or appearing weak. **Misconceptions:** Not fully understanding the importance or feeling undeserving of forgiveness.

4. n/a

5.
Heart Condition: Genuine worship flows from a heart surrendered to God, filled with gratitude and reverence. **Authenticity:** Worship that reflects our true selves, without pretense or performance. **Truth:** Worship that aligns with biblical truth and is led by the Holy Spirit. **Worship:** Worship that extends beyond church gatherings to daily life through obedience and service.
In Matt 15:8-9 it quotes Isaiah warning us about worshipping in vain because the people's hearts are far from God/Jesus.

6.
Acknowledging God's Sovereignty: Recognizing God's authority and wisdom in all aspects of your life. **Seeking Justice and Mercy:** Acting justly and showing mercy toward others that reflects God's character and teaching. **Depending on God:** Trusting in God's provision and guidance rather than relying on our own strength or understanding.

7.
Listening: Valuing others' perspectives and being open to learning from them. **Servanthood:** Putting others' needs before your own and seeking opportunities to serve others. **Admitting Mistakes:** Acknowledging our faults and apologizing when necessary. **Empathy:** Understanding and caring for others' feelings and experiences. **Gratitude:** Recognizing others' contributions and expressing appreciation.

8.
Obedience to Truth: Aligning our actions with God's Word and living according to His principles. **Love:** Loving others genuinely and sacrificially, reflecting God's love for us. **Harmony:** Pursuing unity within the body of Christ through genuine relationships and mutual respect. **Holiness:** Striving for moral purity and integrity in thoughts, words, and deeds, honoring God in every aspect of life.

9.

Some Possibilities: David, Benaiah, Rizpah, Hosea, Shiphrah and Puah, Stephen, Queen Esther, Daniel and friends.

EXAMPLE: Stephen was a devout follower of Jesus, filled with the Holy Spirit. He was chosen to serve the early church in a practical role, distributing food to widows. Yet, his true calling was as a witness to Christ. He displayed extraordinary boldness and courage when confronted by his accusers. He delivered a powerful sermon outlining God's redemptive plan through Israel's history, culminating in Jesus Christ. Despite facing intense opposition and threats, Stephen remained unwavering in his proclamation of the truth.

Lessons we can learn from the life of Stephen:

a) Courage in the face of adversity: Stephen's fearlessness in the face of death is a powerful example of faith in action.

b) Boldness in proclaiming the truth: He didn't shy away from challenging the status quo or confronting his opponents.

c) Focus on God, not self: Stephen's final prayer, forgiving his persecutors, reveals a heart centered on God's love.

Stephen's story is a testament to the transformative power of faith and the courage it can inspire in believers.

10.

The essence of God's character is love and it can be demonstrated tangibly to others through our mercy and compassion. This divine attribute is mirrored in us when we:

Forgive freely: Just as God forgives our sins, extending forgiveness to others demonstrates a heart aligned with God's.

Empathize deeply: Understanding and sharing the feelings of others is a reflection of the compassion of God, who understands our struggles intimately.

Act justly: God is a righteous judge, and our pursuit of fairness and equality mirrors His character.

Love unconditionally: God's love is boundless and without conditions, and when we love others selflessly, we imitate His nature.

Offer grace liberally: As God extends grace to us, offering grace to others allows us to participate in His redemptive work.

SUMMARY: By embodying these qualities, we become living examples of God's love in the world, demonstrating that our hearts are truly connected to His.

11.

Job - Despite losing everything, Job remained faithful to God and experienced restoration (Job 42). **Joseph** - Sold into slavery and wrongly imprisoned, Joseph persevered with integrity and eventually became a ruler in Egypt (Genesis 37-50) where he was ultimately reunited with his family. **David** - Endured persecution and betrayal but remained steadfast in his faith and dependence on God (Psalm 23, 2 Samuel). **Paul** - Faced numerous hardships, including imprisonment and persecution, yet his faith in Christ grew stronger through it all (2 Corinthians 11:23-28). **Daniel** - Resisted compromising his faith despite facing threats and the lion's den, experiencing God's protection and favor (Daniel 1-6). **Moses** - Endured years of hardship and challenges leading the Israelites, relying on God's strength and guidance (Exodus 2-4, Numbers 11-14). **Esther** - Risked her life to save her people, displaying courage and faith in God's providence (Book of Esther). **Ruth** - Endured loss and uncertainty but remained loyal to Naomi and embraced faith in God, leading to blessings (Book of Ruth). **Elijah** - Confronted opposition and experienced God's provision and renewal during his ministry (1 Kings 17-19). **Peter** - Despite his failures and doubts, Peter grew spiritually through repentance and became a bold leader in the early church (Gospels, Acts).

Lesson 5 Do It With *ALL* Your Heart
Q1.
Deuteronomy 4:29
This emphasizes the importance of wholehearted seeking, and the promised result is finding God.
Psalms 119:2
You will be blessed. **LEADER:** You might ask your group how one might expect to be blessed.
Q2.
Old Testament
Deuteronomy 6:4-9
New Testament
Matthew 22:37
This command is extremely important so God not only wants it to come from our heart, but we are to teach it to our children. We should not forget.
Deuteronomy 13:3
God will test you to determine if you really love Him!
Deuteronomy 30:6
God will pave the way by circumcising our hearts so we can truly love Him.
1 Timothy 1:5
The love for God will require a good conscience and sincere faith in order for the heart to be pure enough to love God
1 Peter 1:22
Not only love God, but love one another. See also 1 John 3:19-20a.
Q3.
Deuteronomy 10:12-13
We are commanded to serve.
Deuteronomy 11:13-15 If we obey and serve He will provide. This is a conditional promise.
1 Samuel 12:20, 24-25
If we fear the Lord and serve Him faithfully, we will not be punished.
Q4.
Deuteronomy 26:16
We are commanded to follow God's laws – they should reside in our hearts.
  Dt 6:6 These commandments that I give you today are to be upon your hearts. NIV
  Dt 10:16 Circumcise your hearts, therefore, and do not be stiff-necked any longer. NIV
  Ps 37:31 The law of his God is in his heart; his feet do not slip. NIV
  Ps 40:8I desire to do your will, O my God; your law is within my heart." NIV

Hebrews 8:10 This is the covenant I will make with the house of Israel after that time, declares the Lord. I will put my laws in their minds and write them on their hearts. I will be their God, and they will be my people. NIV
LEADER: You might ask your group what they think it means that the law resides in the heart. Ans: If it's in our heart then we will act accordingly.
Deuteronomy 30:2-3
If we obey God, He will restore us and have compassion on us.
Deuteronomy 30:17-18
God will destroy those who turn to idols.
Proverbs 3:1-2
Obedience will *tend* to produce long life and prosperity.
Q5.
1 Samuel 7:3
We must reject the idols in our lives (anything that is more important than God).
Joel 2:12-13
Fasting, humility, and submission may be required in order to properly repent and sincerely turn toward God and away from sin.
Q6.
Psalms 138:1
David praised and worshipped with all his heart. If that is the way David did it, and he was a man after the heart of God, then that is the way we should do it.
1 Sam 12:20-22
Worship and praise with all your heart. Don't worship worthless idols!
Q7.
Trust in the Lord with all your heart and lean not on your own understanding. Trust and hope in God and God alone! This verse highlights trusting God's wisdom and guidance above our own, emphasizing the importance of wholehearted trust and reliance on God.
Q8.
This verse encourages believers to **do everything wholeheartedly**, as if they were working for the Lord rather than for human masters.
See also Eccl 9:10 that says to work with all our might.
Q9.
Salvation is received by those who truly believe in their heart, not by those who simply say they do.
Q10.
1 Timothy 1:5-7 This passage highlights the goal of the instruction given to believers, which is to *love from a pure heart, a good conscience, and a sincere faith.*
Hebrews 10:22
This verse encourages believers to draw near to God with a true heart and full assurance of faith.
Psalm 51:16-17
 These verses speak of God's approval of sincerity in obedience to His Word, emphasizing that He values a contrite heart.
James 4:8
This verse urges believers to draw near to God with a sincere heart, promising that He will draw near to them.

Make your heart the dwelling place of God.

DISCUSSION QUESTIONS

1.
Loving God with all aspects of our being means prioritizing Him above all else in our lives. It must involve the: **Heart:** Devoting our affections, desires, and passions to God. **Soul:** Surrendering our innermost being and emotions to God's will. **Mind:** Engaging our intellect, thoughts, and understanding in studying His Word and seeking His wisdom. **Strength:** Using our physical abilities and resources to honor God and serve others.

2.
Pursuing God wholeheartedly should influence our decisions and priorities by: **Choices:** Seeking God's guidance in major life decisions and aligning our goals with His will. **Priorities:** Prioritizing spiritual growth, relationships, and service over material pursuits. **Practices:** Integrating prayer, Scripture reading, and worship into our daily routines. **Challenges:** Trusting God in adversity and relying on His strength in all circumstances.

3.
Daily Devotions: Setting aside regular time for prayer and Bible study. **Fellowship:** Engaging in community with other believers for mutual encouragement and accountability. **Service:** Volunteering in church ministries and reaching out to serve those in need. **Meditation:** Reflecting on Scripture and applying its truths to personal life situations. **Obedience:** Willingly obeying God's commands and trusting His guidance in all areas of life. **Spiritual Gifts:** Using the gifts to serve God and His people.

4.
Serving God wholeheartedly is essential because it: **Reflects Love:** Demonstrates our love and devotion to God as His disciples. **Honors God:** Glorifies God by using our gifts and talents for His kingdom purposes. **Builds Character:** Develops humility, compassion, and sacrificial love in our hearts. **Purpose:** Aligns us with God's mission to spread His love and truth to others.

5. n/a

6.
Obedience to God reflects trust and reverence for Him because it: **Shows Submission:** Acknowledges God's authority and sovereignty over our lives. **Demonstrates Faith:** Trusts in God's wisdom and goodness, even when His ways are challenging. **Strengthens Relationship:** Deepens intimacy with God as we align our will with His and experience His faithfulness.
Lack of obedience is more likely a love issue than an obedience problem.

7.
Prayer: Seeking God's strength and guidance in overcoming temptations. **Accountability:** Partnering with trusted friends or mentors for support and encouragement. **Scripture:** Drawing strength from God's Word to resist temptation and make righteous choices. **Repentance:** Confessing and turning away from sin, seeking God's forgiveness and restoration.

8.
Returning to God with all our hearts involves: **Repentance:** Genuine sorrow for straying from God's will and turning back to Him. **Renewal:** Reaffirming commitment to God's ways through prayer, confession, and seeking His guidance. **Restoration:** Experiencing God's forgiveness and grace, allowing Him to heal and transform our hearts. Success requires commitment and

intentionality – see Appendix B.

9.

(a) Calm: Trusting God during times of peace involves resting in His sovereignty and goodness, knowing He holds my future in His hands.

(b) Uncertainty: In uncertain times, trusting God brings peace by relying on His promises and believing He works all things for our good (Romans 8:28).

10.

Bringing God into your work involves: **Integrity:** Conducting yourselves with honesty and integrity, reflecting God's character. **Service:** Viewing work as an opportunity to serve God and others, striving for excellence in all tasks. Being diligent. **Relationships:** Treating coworkers and employers with respect and kindness, demonstrating Christ's love in actions and attitudes.

Lesson 6 Encountering the Divine
DISCUSSION QUESTIONS

1.

Having a personal encounter with Jesus or God means experiencing a profound interaction where one senses the presence, love, and transformative power of God in a deeply personal way. It may involve a spiritual awakening or realization of God's reality and relevance in one's life. It could manifest itself in dramatic changes in behavior.

2.

Each encountered Jesus personally, which challenged their previous beliefs and lifestyles. Paul's encounter on the road to Damascus transformed him from a persecutor to a missionary. Peter's encounters deepened his faith and leadership role. Zacchaeus' encounter led to repentance and a commitment to justice.

3. n/a

4.

Knowing about Jesus intellectually involves understanding facts, whereas encountering Jesus is a personal, transformative experience that affects beliefs, attitudes, and actions. It's a heart-to-heart connection rather than just head knowledge. An encounter will normally cause one to take some type of action.

5.

The woman encountered Jesus intimately, experiencing His wisdom, sovereignty, and foreknowledge. Her story teaches us about grace and the transformative power of encountering Jesus in our sinfulness.

6.

Pride, fear of change, and cultural or religious barriers can hinder seeking after God. Misconceptions about who Jesus is and skepticism about His relevance today, can also be obstacles. Or, just the fact that others might discover their interest in spiritual questions could cause some to shrink back.

7.

Encountering Jesus can provide perspective, strength, courage, or peace. Jesus can offer hope and guidance through life's trials.

8.

Both were Gentiles who encountered God's grace through Jesus. Their stories show God's inclusive love and His power to transform hearts, regardless of background or status.

9.

Encountering Jesus fosters love, forgiveness, and compassion, transforming relationships with humility and grace. It motivates us to reflect His love to everyone we encounter. It often changes our priorities and behaviors.

10. n/a

11.

We could practice some of the spiritual disciplines like:

Inward Disciplines

Prayer: Communing with God through spoken or silent conversation.

Meditation: Focusing the mind on spiritual truths, often involving Scripture.

Fasting: Abstaining from food or other desires for spiritual focus.

Study: Diligent exploration of Scripture and theological topics.

Outward Disciplines

Simplicity: Living a life free from material possessions and distractions.

Solitude: Spending time alone with God.

Submission: Yielding one's life to God's will.

Service: Serving others as an expression of love for God.

Corporate Disciplines

Confession: Acknowledging sins to God and others.

Worship: Praising and honoring God through music, prayer, and Scripture.

Guidance: Seeking wisdom and direction from God and others.

Celebration: Sharing in the joy of God's presence and work.

12.

Encountering Jesus challenges worldly values like materialism, importance of self, and selfishness. In crises, faith in Jesus provides peace and strength, offering hope and guiding decisions with wisdom.

An encounter with Jesus today would undoubtedly disrupt the status quo, challenging many of our deeply entrenched cultural and societal values.

Challenge to Individualism: Jesus emphasized community and interdependence. This contrasts sharply with our culture's focus on individual achievement and self-reliance. His teaching on caring for the poor would challenge our consumerism and materialism.

Challenge to Materialism: Jesus lived a simple life and encouraged His followers to do the same. This directly contradicts our culture's obsession with wealth and possessions. His emphasis on giving and helping the needy would again challenge our consumerist mindset and prioritization of personal gain.

Challenge to Power Structures: Jesus overturned societal power structures by embracing humility and service. This would challenge our admiration for authority and status. His advocacy for the needy, marginalized, and oppressed would conflict with systemic inequalities and injustices that exist today.

Challenge to Moral Relativism: Jesus offered absolute moral truths, challenging the postmodern emphasis on subjective morality. His teachings on forgiveness and reconciliation contradict our culture's focus on retribution and revenge.

CONCLUSION: Ultimately, an encounter with Jesus would require a radical shift in worldview and priorities. It would challenge us to question our values, relationships, and our understanding of success and fulfillment.

Lesson 7 The Blind Man

1.

(1) Sin is in the world because of the Fall. (2) Bad things happen because of sin in the world, in man, and in Satan. (3) God used the man's blindness to display His power, grace, and mercy, bringing glory to Himself. **LEADER:** You might ask, "Does this say God caused the blindness. Ans: No

2.

(1) They were very confused! (2) This was a strange and supernatural event! (3) Note: the learned Pharisees turned to an unlearned man and asked him to explain what happened. (4) The real question is, "What do you say about Him?"

3.

(1) He had definitely been born blind. (2) Concerning his ability to see: "Ask him – he was the one who was healed. He is of age!" (3) They were likely afraid that they might lose standing with their family and friends, particularly if they got on the wrong side of the debate. They were also concerned that they would be excommunicated, which would cut them off from their Jewish community.

4.

(1) He put them on the defensive. (2) He became boldly aggressive. **LEADER:** You might ask your group, "Do you think the blind man had the right to boldly challenge them or did he cross the line in 9:27. Ans: He's at least close to the line with his attitude and tone.

5.

(1) It sounds like a comedy routine. (2) It's almost ridiculous when you consider it is an exchange between an uneducated beggar and Pharisees, who were experts in the Law.

6.

The blind man is arguing very clearly and logically that Jesus has to be from God. Interestingly the blind man is uneducated and the Pharisees are supposed to be learned.

7.

(1) They didn't really answer. (2) They probably didn't have an answer, so they attacked his character and insulted him. Does that sound familiar? (3) Their position was that he was sinful, and therefore worthless. (4) They considered his opinion to be of no value. If you can't answer questions then attack and ridicule the person. Attack the messenger.

8.

9:11   a man

9:17   a prophet

9:27   had disciples (implying a teacher or prophet)

9:33   one from God

9:38   Lord, to be worshipped

9.

Progressive revelation by the Holy Spirit. **LEADER:** You might ask, "Compare this to how your understanding of Jesus has advanced since you first heard of Him." Encourage your group to share their stories. Maybe tell a bit of your own story to encourage others to speak.

10.

He asserts that God doesn't answer the prayers of sinners. (1) God does not answer prayer for those involved in unbelief, idolatry, or deliberate and continual sin. (2) This is <u>not</u> absolute because God will always respond to true repentance and a request for forgiveness. (3) Why would God answer our prayers and do what we ask if we refuse to do what He asks?

SIDE NOTE: We know that in general the blind man was correct. The Bible says that God does not "listen" to sinners, meaning He would not normally respond or answer their prayers. This is confirmed in other passages:

<u>Psalm 66:17-18</u> I cried to him with my mouth, and high praise was on my tongue. 18 If I had cherished iniquity in my heart, the Lord would not have listened. ESV

<u>Proverbs 28:9</u> If one turns away his ear from hearing the law, even his prayer is an abomination. ESV

<u>1 Peter 3:7</u> Likewise, husbands, live with your wives in an understanding way, showing honor to the woman as the weaker vessel, since they are heirs with you of the grace of life, so that your prayers may not be hindered. ESV

<u>James 4:3</u> You ask and do not receive, because you ask wrongly, to spend it on your passions. ESV

11.

(1) Meaning: Removed from participation in the synagogue and/or temple, even shunned by the community. (2) It probably was not a true excommunication because it did not seem to follow any rules and procedures, but in practice had the same impact. (3) It is also very difficult to know what the rules and process for excommunication were at this time. The historical writings do not give us a clear picture of what was meant by excommunication. (4) The leaders were angry so they just ignored any rules that might have existed and removed him. (5) Whether their rash actions held up over time is unknown.

12. n/a

13.

LEADER, give your group time to share. It may be difficult for some to voice their doubts or describe what they do not understand.

14.

The story of the man born blind is a stark reminder of the dangers of spiritual blindness. The Pharisees, despite their religious knowledge, were unable to perceive the divine work of God before their eyes.

Lessons we can learn from this encounter with Jesus:
Guard against spiritual pride: We must be ever vigilant against the temptation to believe we are spiritually superior to others. Humility is essential.
Prioritize open hearts: A closed heart is resistant to truth. We should cultivate a heart open to God's revelation and the experiences of others.
Beware of tradition: While traditions can be valuable, they should never replace or hinder a personal relationship with Jesus.
Seek truth: Like the healed man, we should pursue truth diligently, even when it challenges our preconceived notions.
Be witnesses: Just as the healed man became a witness to Jesus, we should be willing to share our faith and experiences with others.
Conclusion: Ultimately, the Pharisees' failure to believe in Jesus highlights the importance of a genuine heart transformation. It is not enough to simply know the truth; we must receive it with faith and allow it to change us from within.

Lesson 8 Crippled Man at Lystra
DISCUSSION QUESTIONS

1.
Paul wanted answers to several questions: a) Was he a fake? b) Did he really want to be healed? c) Did he have any faith? d) The NIV says, "*Paul looked directly at him and saw that he had faith to be healed.*"

2.
Paul made the point that in this case faith played a role in the healing.
LEADER: Don't be tempted to generalize that every healing involves faith or that those who are not healed have insufficient faith.

3.
(1) Possibly. The real issue that Paul was probably trying to determine was, "Is this man's faith real?" One might easily say, "I have faith," or "I believe," but it is not real. The words are spoken to obtain the desired result, rather than a testimony of true faith. (2) This might be compared to the demons who know who Jesus is, but reject Him and follow Satan. (3) This reference probably means that the crippled man had faith in Jesus as Lord, not that he had some level of superior faith.

4.
(1) Probably supernatural revelation that allowed Paul to know. (2) It probably does not mean he actually "saw" something in the man.

5.
(1) No atrophy – he jumped up and immediately walked around. (2) it implies a natural walk – no limping, no shuffling. (3) He had the strength to jump up and walk immediately. (4) Normally, people who are injured require months to learn to walk again.

6.
(1) They shouted in their language, "The gods have come down to us in the likeness of men!" (2) WHY: (a) It was a true healing. (b) The crowd knew this

man and they knew he had been crippled. (c) Since they knew the man, it had to be a miracle that only a god could perform.

7.

(1) No, they knew nothing of the one true God. (2) Ancient legends in Lystra told of Zeus and Hermes visiting the city of Lystra but nobody recognized them (except one old couple). This may have been a reaction to make sure the same thing did not happen again. (2) The reaction about the identity of Paul and Barnabas as Greek gods is not surprising because that is all the people knew. (3) Historically the major problem with the Jewish faith was idol worship and false gods.

8.

(1) Brought bulls and wreaths to the city gate in order to sacrifice them to Paul and Barnabas because he believed they were gods. (2) Paul and Barnabas must have been pretty impressive to this priest.

9.

(1) The priest himself also wanted to sacrifice! (2) He probably did not even witness the healing! (3) He may have recognized that the healing was real. (4) The people may have told him about Paul.

10.

(1) They tore their clothes. (2) This demonstrated great concern, or great anguish. (3) They also rushed into the crowd to correct the misunderstanding.

11.

(1) Worthless. (2) "Worthless things" probably indicated false gods. (3) 1 Samuel 12:20-21 *Samuel replied, "Don't be afraid. Even though you have committed all this evil, don't turn away from following the Lord. Instead, worship the Lord with all your heart. 21 Don't turn away to follow worthless things that can't profit or deliver you; they are worthless."* (HCSB)

12.

(1) Some were totally convinced. (2) Some still wanted to offer sacrifices to Paul and Barnabas. THEN, when the Jews from Antioch and Iconium arrived the crowd was won over to the side of the visiting Jews – that didn't take long!

LEADER: You might ask your group how the crowd (local people) were won over to the visiting Jews so quickly.

Ignorance and Superstition: The people of Lystra were steeped in pagan beliefs and superstitions. The miraculous healing of a lifelong cripple was a phenomenon outside their realm of understanding. Given their worldview, attributing such a feat to divine intervention was a logical conclusion.

Culture: Lystra likely had a history of legends and myths involving divine beings appearing in human form. The idea of gods visiting their people was not entirely foreign to them.

Desperate Need: The people of Lystra, like many, were searching for answers to life's challenges and a sense of hope. A miraculous healing offered a tangible manifestation of divine power and a potential solution to their problems.

Psychological Impact: Witnessing a seemingly impossible event can be emotionally overwhelming. The crowd's excitement and fervor were likely heightened by the sheer wonder of what they had witnessed.

It's important to note that this initial reverence was short-lived. Once the truth about Paul and Barnabas was revealed, the crowd's attitude shifted dramatically. This underscores the ephemeral nature of such emotional responses and the importance of genuine faith based on solid understanding.
13.
(1) They turned Paul's claims that he was not a god against him. (2) They admitted or claimed not to be gods. (3) Paul told them to turn away from their "false" gods. Thus, they denigrated the people's gods. (4) They had other gods that provided rain, food, etc. Those things were not coming from Yahweh. (5) They used the same false testimony claimed in Iconium (14:2) to poison the minds of the people. (6) This would probably have been easy once the people were no longer reacting emotionally.

14. n/a

15.

The outcome of their encounter with the people of Lystra could have been drastically different. Here are some potential consequences:

False Worship: Without a strong foundation in truth, they might have been tempted to accept the adoration of the crowd and embrace the false worship offered to them as gods. This would have led to spiritual compromise, departure, or total destruction of their mission.

Fear and Retreat: Facing the imminent threat of stoning, a lack of faith could have caused them to flee in fear, abandoning the people of Lystra without providing further spiritual guidance or support.

Compromise: Without a deep conviction in the gospel, they might have watered down their message to appease the crowd or avoid persecution, thereby compromising the truth.

Loss of Impact: A wavering faith would have diminished their authority and credibility, hindering their ability to effectively share the gospel and establish churches.

FINAL DISCUSSION QUESTION

(a) The response of the people

The people of Lystra, upon witnessing the miraculous healing of the crippled man, immediately attributed divine status to Paul and Barnabas. This reaction reveals a deep-seated spiritual hunger and a longing for a higher power. However, their understanding of the divine was clouded by their pagan beliefs and cultural context. They lacked a true knowledge of the one true God and His nature. This encounter demonstrates the importance of:

Accurate biblical teaching: People need to be instructed in the true nature of God and His plan for humanity.

Discernment: True faith requires discernment to differentiate between genuine divine power and false manifestations.

(b) The response of the leaders

The subsequent stoning of Paul highlights the opposition that often arises when the truth challenges established religious and societal norms. The leaders, influenced by religious and cultural prejudices, rejected the message of Christ and resorted to violence to silence it. This demonstrates the need for:

Open-mindedness: Leaders, both religious and secular, should be open to new truths and perspectives.

Perseverance: Those who proclaim the gospel must be prepared to face opposition and remain steadfast in their faith.

Wisdom: Understanding the cultural and religious context is essential for effective communication of the gospel.

Conclusion: the events in Acts 14 emphasize the critical role of heart knowledge and understanding in having genuine faith. While miraculous signs can attract attention, it is the transformative power of the gospel that truly changes lives.

Free PDF
MAKE WISE DECISIONS

[Get the ebook version for 99 cents]

Consequences Shape Lives.

This book discusses the nature of decisions and explores eight essential questions to make better decisions.

You are a few decisions away from transforming your life. You can make better decisions! This resource has sections on what makes a poor decision, questions to ask yourself, traps to avoid, short and sweet decisions, the wise decision framework, and twenty ways to be wise. It also has a handy decision-making checklist. (12 pages)

Free PDF: https://getwisdompublishing.com/resource-registration/

Kindle ebook for 99 cents: https://www.amazon.com/dp/B0FG8NC53J

Ebook

Free PDF

Ten Steps to Wise Choices

Timeless Wisdom. Practical Tools. Lasting Impact.

Free PDF
Life Improvement Principles
[Get the ebook version for 99 cents]

You can live your best life!

Welcome to a journey of discovery! In case you have forgotten, your actions have consequences. Unlock your potential! This book (60+ pages) provides the overview of all our strategies and wisdom principles to live your best life. You *can* transform your life! Get your wisdom-based roadmap to a better life and unlock all the possibilities for growth and success.

Free PDF: https://getwisdompublishing.com/resource-registration/

Kindle ebook for 99 cents:
https://www.amazon.com/dp/B0FG883KZM

Ebook

Free PDF

Make it your life goal to be the best you can be!

Discover Wisdom and live the life you deserve.

What Next?

Continue Your Journey

Continue Study in the *Jesus Follower* Series

The Jesus Follower Bible Study Series
https://www.amazon.com/dp/B0DHP39P5J

Be Challenged by the *OBSCURE* Series

The *OBSCURE* Bible Study Series
https://www.amazon.com/dp/B08T7TL1B1

Tackle Wisdom-Driven Life Change

Apply Biblical Wisdom to Live Your Best Life!
"Effective Life Change"
https://www.amazon.com/dp/1952359732

Know What You Should Pray

Personal Daily Prayer Guide
https://www.amazon.com/What-Should-Pray-Personal-Journal/dp/1952359260/

Decide to be the Very Best You Can Be

The Life Planning Series
https://www.amazon.com/dp/B09TH9SYC4

__You Can Help:__
SOCIAL MEDIA: Mention The Jesus Follower Bible Study Series on your social platforms. Include the hashtag #jesusbiblestudy so we are aware of your post.

FRIENDS: Recommend this series to your family, friends, small group, Sunday School class leaders, or your church.

REVIEW: Please give us your honest review at
https://www.amazon.com/dp/1952359716

Make your heart the dwelling place of God.

The OBSCURE Bible Study Series

**Continue your journey through the hidden
wisdom of Scripture with the OBSCURE Series.**

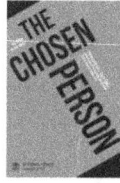

Blasphemy, Grace, Quarrels & Reconciliation: The lives of first-century disciples.
This book presents Joseph of Arimathea, Joanna, Ananias, Hymenaeus, and Cornelius (a centurion). It illustrates the nature and challenges of life as a first-century disciple.

The Beginning and the End: From creation to eternity.
This book has four lessons from Genesis and four from Revelation covering creation, rebellion, grace, worship, and eternity. God is leading us to worship in the Throne Room.

God at the Center: He is sovereign and I am not.
This book examines the virgin birth, worship, prayer, the sovereignty of God, compromise, and trust. God is at the center of all these stories. He is at the center of our lives.

Women of Courage: God did some serious business with these women.
This book examines the lives of Jael, Rizpah, the woman of Tekoa, Tabitha, Shiphrah, and Lydia. These women exhibit great courage and faithfulness. God used them in amazing ways.

The Beginning of Wisdom: Your personal character counts.
In this book we find courage, loyalty, thankfulness, love, forgiveness, and humility. Personal character counts. Decisions have consequences. Wisdom will help us stand firm in our faith.

Miracles & Rebellion: The good, the bad, and the indifferent.
God hates sin and loves to heal the faithful. The rebellion of Korah, Haman, and Alexander compare to the healing stories of Aeneas, a slave girl, and the crippled man at Lystra.

The Chosen People: There is a remnant.
This book concentrates mostly on Israel in the Old Testament, but also covers some interesting subjects as Lucifer, Michael the archangel, and Job's wife.

The Chosen Person: Keep your eyes on Jesus.
The focus is on Jesus and the superiority of Christ. We investigate Melchizedek, the disciples on the road to Emmaus, Nicodemus, and the criminal on the cross.

WEBSITE: http://getwisdompublishing.com/products/
AMAZON: www.amazon.com/author/stephenhberkey

Life Planning Series

Read these books if you want to live a better life.
The primary audience for this series is the secular self-help market,
but the concepts are Christian based.

CHOOSE FAITH	**For the spiritual seeker and those with spiritual questions.** *Your Spiritual Guidebook For Questions About Religion, God, Heaven, Truth, Evil, and the Afterlife.* https://www.amazon.com/dp/1952359473
CHOOSE CORE VALUES	**Core values will drive your life.** https://www.amazon.com/dp/195235949X

Other Titles in the Life Planning Series
CHOOSE Integrity
CHOOSE Friends Wisely
CHOOSE The Right Words
CHOOSE Good Work Habits
CHOOSE Financial Responsibility
CHOOSE A Positive Self-Image
CHOOSE Leadership
CHOOSE Love and Family
LIFE PLANNING HANDBOOK A Life Plan Is The Key To Personal Growth https://www.amazon.com/gp/product/1952359325

Go to:

https://www.amazon.com/dp/B09TH9SYC4

to get your copy.

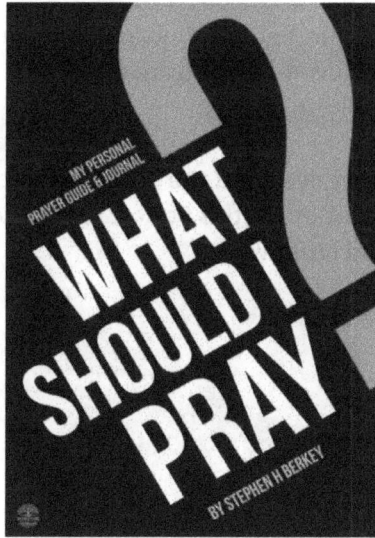

Acknowledgments

My wife has patiently persevered while I indulged my interest in writing. Thank you for all your help and assistance.

Our older daughter has been an invaluable resource. She has also graciously produced our website at www.getwisdompublishing.com

Our middle daughter designed the covers for most of my books, but I gave her a vacation on this Series. We are very grateful for her help, talent and creativity.

Notes

None

About the Author

Steve attended church as a child and accepted Christ when he was 10 years old. But his walk with Jesus left a lot to be desired for the next 44 years. In 1994 he "wrestled" with God for some period of months and in September of that year totally surrendered his life to Jesus.

In 1996 he was so driven to study God's Word that he attended the Indianapolis campus of Trinity Evangelical Divinity School (Chicago) to earn a Certificate of Biblical Studies. His hunger for God's Word led him to lead and write all his own Bible studies for his small group. He has been a Bible study leader for the past 25 years.

After 25 years as an actuary, and 20 years as an entrepreneur, he began his third career as an author in 2020, when he published The OBSCURE Bible Study Series. The Jesus Follower Bible Study Series was completed in early 2025. He is a member of The Church at Station Hill in Spring Hill, TN, a regional campus of Brentwood Baptist (Brentwood TN).

"Get Wisdom Publishing is dedicated to being the trusted source of wisdom-driven books that inspire growth, guide decisions, and empower readers to live with purpose and fulfillment."

Contact Us

Website: www.getwisdompublishing.com

Email: info@getwisdompublishing.com

Facebook: Get Wisdom Publishing

Author's Page:
www.amazon.com/author/stephenhberkey

Amazon's Jesus Follower Bible Study Series page:
https://www.amazon.com/dp/B0DHP39P5J

"Go beyond devotionals.
Experience biblical wisdom in action!"

GETWISDOM
PUBLISHING

www.ingramcontent.com/pod-product-compliance
Lightning Source LLC
Chambersburg PA
CBHW060322050426
42449CB00011B/2606